The Shepherd's Guidebook

The Shepherd's Guidebook

*Spiritual and Practical Foundations
for Cell Group Leaders*

Revised Edition

Ralph W. Neighbour Jr.

TOUCH Outreach Ministries
Houston, TX 77079

The Shepherd's Guidebook
Revised Edition

Special thanks to Dr. Joe McKeever for many of the illustrations.

ISBN No. 1-880828-86-3
Dewey Decimal Classification Number: 248.4
Subject Heading: CHRISTIAN LIFE

AVAILABLE FROM:
Touch Outreach Ministries
P. O. Box 19888
Houston, TX 77079
Tel.: 1-800-735-5865
Fax: 713-497-0904

Touch Resource
3, Marine Parade Central
Singapore 1544
Tel.: 65-440-7544
Fax: 65-440-4586

Touch International (SA)
P. O. Box 1223
Newcastle 2940
ASA
Tel.: (03431) 28111
Fax: (03431) 24211

A  Module

Printed in Singapore

Contents

Preface 7

Part One: The Shepherd's Life
1. Welcome to the Life of a Shepherd! 13
2. The Qualities of a Good Shepherd 23
3. The Shepherd as an Equipper 35

Part Two: The Shepherd's Tasks
4. As You Go, Develop Apprentices! 45
5. Equipping the Flock for Ministry 51
6. The "Year of Equipping" 61
7. The Journey Guide 67
8. The Shepherd's Prayer Life 73
9. "Kinning:" Creating Christian Kinfolk 87
10. Reaching the Unreached 95
11. Caring: A Work of Tender Love 109
12. Will the Little Children Suffer? 121
13. Too Much Month at the End of the Money 135

Part Three: Shepherding Your Cell Group
14. How Cell Groups Function 147
15. Having Meaningful Gatherings 157
16. Leading the Flock to Experience God 169
17. Critical Moments in Cell Group Life 179
18. Get Acquainted Activities 185

Part Four: Twelve Cell Group Gatherings
19. Cell Group Sessions 191

Part Five: Shepherding Tools
20. Journey Guide Helps 221
21. Useful Forms 237

Glossary 251

Dedication

To all the young men who dream dreams . . .
And to the older men who, like myself, keep seeing visions . . .
To those who believe "Clergy" is a word to be replaced by "Equipper" . . .

To the young pastor and his wife who have just opted out of the traditional church and have said to each other, "Pastoring like this is just not worth it!"

To Ben Wong in Hong Kong; to Dion Robert in Abidjan; to Gerald Martin and Larry Stockstill in the United States; to Sergio Solorzano in El Salvador; to Jon Vande Reit in Moscow; to Martin Hopkins in South Africa, and the hundreds and hundreds of church planters and pastors who have launched into the Cell Church world since the first edition of this book was released.

But especially to
Lawrence Khong,

Who has grasped the vision of the Cell Church as no other man I know, and to whom I shall be forever indebted for the privilege of working at his side. I have served as his tutor; he has been my shepherd as no other man. I thank God upon every remembrance of him.

Preface to
the Revised Edition

This guidebook has taken twenty-nine years to write. That's how long I have been searching for the answers to the misery found in traditional church structures. During a part of that period, I pastored a church which sought to pioneer in small group lifestyles. I was as a blind man leading the blind, for there were no models for us to follow. I wish this book had existed when I was thirty-six, starting that journey. I would have devoured its pages. But few others would have read it, and no publisher would have risked the financial loss of publishing it!

Back then, only a few plucky fellows had left traditionalism behind to experiment. Most of us were considered too innovative for our age. Larry Richards and others like him were fellow travelers in those early days, and we clung to each other out of necessity. The conception of Cells being the basic building block of church life had not yet developed, nor had their union to form Congregations evolved. Praise as a worship form for Celebrations was also an unborn child.

The Holy Spirit of God has now formed the lovely Bride of Christ in a more biblical way. The explosion of Cell Group Churches around the world is absolutely awesome! My book, *Where Do We Go From Here?* has now been translated into many languages and has been read by tens of thousands. I wrote it to tell the story of the lovely Bride and give practical guidance to newcomers. It tells the broader story, and provides a wider understanding of how Cell Groups fit into the overall life of the Cell Church than does this book.

This is a handbook. It is intended for use in Cell Churches, not traditional ones. For ten years I sought to bring renewal to the traditional church. I distributed over ten thousand copies of *Touch Basic Training* and taught over seven hundred pastors of traditional churches to use relational Share Groups to evangelize the lost. Most of those men found it impossible to add evangelistic Share Groups to the cluttered programs of their church. Twenty-three of them were released by their congregations for trying to insert Share Groups into church life.

I have come to a conclusion: you cannot put new wine into old skins! I would hope that you will understand this, and not attempt to mix this oil with the tepid water of traditional church structures. This guidebook is not written to renew existing church structures. I have written it for the thousands of Christian communities who have finally said, "Out with traditional church life! We won't renew anything; we will be as new as the first century church."

Around the world, these new Cell Churches far outstrip the growth seen using traditional church programs like Sunday School. More and more Christian workers are recognizing the leukemia in old systems of church life. Look at the thirty-three per cent of these churches which have never grown beyond fifty members, and at another thirty-three per cent which stopped growing at one hundred fifty, and another twenty-eight per cent which stalled at three hundred fifty, and at the five per cent which rarely grow beyond two thousand, and ask, "Why? What makes them quit growing?"

They are an embarrassment when compared to the growth of the early church, which exploded from 120 souls to blanket the Roman Empire in sixty years! And they are mocked by the recent development of Cell Churches around the world which often reach tens of thousands in hostile environments.

Have I said it pointedly enough? I am not writing this for faint-hearted pastors such as the one I met recently who said to me, "Korea's culture suits the Cell Church. Cell Groups won't work in the United States." This ridiculous comment is frequently made by clergymen who sleep while Satan neutralizes the Body of Christ.

I have struggled with the use of the name "Shepherd" as my description of a Cell Leader in this book. The term fell into disrepute because of a charismatic group which created "control groups," using the word "Shepherd" in their nomenclature. They required the "flock" to tithe directly to their "Shepherd," who in turn sent a percentage of the income to the "Apostle" who was over them all. Cell Churches do not use this distorted concept. True community will help each Christian grow and reach the greatest independence possible.

Therefore, I have chosen to stick with the term, feeling that this group does not deserve the right to rob an entire generation of God's people of their rightful use of a biblical word. A Shepherd is not a person who lords over others, controlling them by directives and permissions granted. A true Shepherd will live with the flock, virtually unseen much of the time, rejoicing that the brothers and sisters are developing in faith and ministry.

A true Cell Group finds itself suspended between two poles, each influencing its lifestyle. The first pole is a compelling desire to bear witness to its life in Christ. The members have good news to offer others, news which can bring happiness, truth, and fulfillment. They want to be lights on a hill, shining into the darkness. They stand ready to multiply when they reach fifteen members, knowing that this is the logical result of reaching out and to grow beyond that figure is to kill the group.

In this mode, they are fighting comrades in a war against Satan's power. If you have skepticism about the reality of Satan and demonic forces, you need to rethink your position. Bringing unbelievers to Christ is not a matter of chanting a carefully memorized "database" of scripture verses, but rather of snatching brands from the burning. Bearing witness will call forth the demons of hell to attack the flock. Be prepared!

The second pole which influences the lifestyle of the group is the quality of relationships. Finding unity with others, discovering the "why" of life together, being bound in friendship, are indescribable treasures. It is in the Cell Group that each person discovers they have value, that they are loveable and that they can love. The message of Jesus calls us to live together in a special way as a community of the redeemed.

Both poles must remain equally strong in shaping the group! The worldwide tendency of Christian Cells is to eliminate evangelism and simply "nurture" one another. Such Cells create ossified people who are best described as "navel gazing believers." No true discipleship ever takes place when believers focus on one another while ignoring the suffering world around them.

Pastor Yaye Dione Robert is a glorious study of a man with a Shepherd's heart. He began his ministry in Abidjan, Ivory Coast, with three persons in 1976. As of April, 1994, there were over 45,000 members in his Cell Church. Most Cells, similar to the Cell Groups described in this book, multiply in about three months' time.

Literally thousands are being swept into the Kingdom each year by this African movement of men and women who live together and reach out to others. The tension between the two poles of equipping and outreach is just right, and God adds daily to their number.

Some special conditions have to be met if the life of the Cell Group is to deepen and grow through all the crises, tensions and good times. If these conditions aren't met, every sort of deviation is possible. Many traditional churches have tried groups as a "gimmick" to provide growth or nurture, only to discover they have brought spiritual decline to the members instead.

For that reason, it is important for the potential Shepherd to read this manual prayerfully, absorbing key thoughts as the Holy Spirit sheds insights into the local situation. The last sections of the book provide helpful forms and guidelines for weekly Cell Group meetings.

This revision is being prepared in Singapore in 1994. I have served for several years beside my dear friend, Lawrence Khong, as we have launched a Cell Church which is now passing the 6,000 mark in seven years. We have learned many lessons together about what it takes to grow a Cell Church. In addition to my books, we are currently producing instructional videotapes and conducting Cell Church conferences around the world. The *Cell Church Magazine* now shares information about the movement. You are encouraged to write to us at the addresses on the copyright page for additional information.

The copyright on this book is only to insure that some unscrupulous person will not republish parts of it for resale. However, permission is hereby granted to reproduce all forms, rewrite chapters to better equip your Cell Leaders, and mix my text with your own ideas. If just one additional soul can be brought into the Kingdom through adapting this material to better fit your situation, do it!

Would you write to me after you have used this book? Let's share in further revisions of it for the generations of Cell Churches who will follow us. And remember: "He is no fool who gives what he cannot keep to gain what he cannot lose."

Ralph W. Neighbour, Jr.
Box 19888
Houston, TX, 77224, U.S.A.

Part One

The Shepherd's Life

1

Welcome to the Life of a Shepherd!

WELCOME TO YOUR MINISTRY, SHEPHERD! The Cell Church is a New Testament form of church life. To understand it, think of the human body. Cells are its basic building blocks. Without cells, it wouldn't even exist! Some cells combine to form bones. Others cluster to become blood, organs, eyes, skin, etc.

The basic building block of a Cell Church is a Cell: a community of 7-15 persons, moving constantly from house to house for its activities. Within these Cells, the church exists in a pure first century form. Sometimes these Cells are called "Basic Christian Communities." The name they are called isn't important, but the fact that the Cells are the basic building blocks of the church is vital!

There is a heaven and earth difference between a church *with* Cells and a Cell Church. The first has a lot of programs to occupy believers. The second fits everything the church does into a Cell Group structure. It has no programs—only Cells.

The Cell Group is the place where people are evangelized, nurtured, equipped to serve, and where members build up (edify) one another. It is a community where believers are called to be accountable and totally transparent with one another.

Because the Cell meets all the basic needs of the believer, it replaces the array of programs which are conducted by traditional churches. The pure Cell Church has no Sunday School, Training Hour, Visitation Night, Midweek Service, or any of the other formal services which comprise traditional church calendars. In place of this, each Cell becomes a true community, an "extended family unit." A pure Cell Church sees no need for other programs. All its basic needs are met in the Cell Groups. Adding further programs to its church life dissipates the focus of believers and becomes counter-productive.

There are limits to the activities within a Cell Group. While it may begin its sessions with a brief time of praise and worship, that is not its primary purpose. While it may use the Bible freely in its lifestyle, it is not a place for Bible Study. These needs are fulfilled at a different level in the life of the church, as we shall see in the paragraphs which follow. Thus, it is not necessary for the Cell Leader to be a great Bible teacher, or even a strong communicator.

Instead, he or she must be a Shepherd with a love for the members of the Cell Group. As a Shepherd cares for the sheep and ministers to their needs, so a Shepherd serves on a pastoral level. Caring for the needs of the Cell Group members and leading them into ministry is his or her passion.

It will make a great difference in your ministry if you will read this book with that concept clearly fixed in your mind. A Cell Leader assumes a pastoral role; shepherding is the ministry God has assigned to you.

SHEPHERD, YOUR MINISTRY IS VITAL!

In Matthew 9:36, Jesus saw crowds of people in the Jewish community and "had compassion on them, because they were harassed and helpless, like sheep without a shepherd." Today, the same problem exists in the Christian community. In the traditional church, a paid pastoral staff is employed to do the work of a shepherd. Usually one pastor is responsible for dozens or even hundreds of Christians. It is impossible for one shepherd to care for so many sheep. Little attention can be devoted to their spiritual and personal needs. As a result, large numbers of believers are delinquent members of their churches and undeveloped for ministry to others!

In the Cell Church, that does not happen! The ratio of shepherds to sheep is never allowed to exceed a ratio of 1:15. Thus, the needs of the flock can be closely observed. The spiritual gifts of each person can be developed. Each Cell member becomes a point of witness to others.

Do not perceive yourself as equivalent to a Sunday School teacher who presents a lesson to a small group. Do not see yourself as a "church worker" operating a small group. You are a Shepherd!

You will perform many pastoral functions. In many Cell Churches around the world, the Shepherd (Cell Leader) baptizes converts, serves the Lord's Supper, and prays for the sick. As a Shepherd, you are the first level of pastoral care for your Cell Group members.

A TYPICAL CELL GROUP

Study the following diagram carefully.

Three Groups Will Be In Your Flock (See 1 John 2:13-14)

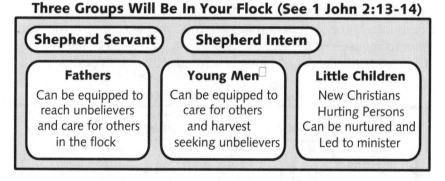

Shepherd Servant	Shepherd Intern	
Fathers	**Young Men**	**Little Children**
Can be equipped to reach unbelievers and care for others in the flock	Can be equipped to care for others and harvest seeking unbelievers	New Christians Hurting Persons Can be nurtured and Led to minister

The three divisions shown describe three subgroups within your Cell Group. You may have to decide how to classify the members of your flock as you get to know them—and reclassify them as they mature in their spiritual journey. These three levels of maturity are alluded to in 1 John 2:13-14. The terms "fathers" and "young men" refer to both men and women.

Your Cell Group will include:
• A SHEPHERD (Cell Leader). You are responsible for the pastoral care of the flock.
• A SHEPHERD INTERN, who will be at your side all of the time. In about six months, your Cell Group will multiply. Half of them will

stay with you, the other half will be shepherded by the Intern. At that time, each of you will develop new Interns.

FIVE TO SEVEN PEOPLE, who will form the Cell Group. As you get to know them, you will find they are all at different mileposts on their journey towards maturity. Of course, it's impossible to divide everyone into neat boxes, but you will probably recognize they will fall into these general areas:

1. LITTLE CHILDREN: New Christians, who need to be nurtured with the "milk of the Word," along with Hurting Persons. These are believers who require inner healing for past hurts before there will be any further growth.

2. YOUNG MEN: Believers who have revised their value systems and are ready to share their faith with others.

3. FATHERS: Committed servants, who can be equipped to penetrate the unchurched and help you with the care of the rest of the flock.

Little Children need to be sponsored by the Young Men for nurture. Young Men need to be linked to Fathers who can guide them into higher levels of ministry. Your Shepherd Intern will learn how to minister to the Hurting Persons as part of his or her training. Thus, a spiritual chain of caring is formed within the flock.

A Cell Group Has Two Ways Of Reaching Out

Shepherd Servant	Shepherd Intern	
Fathers	**Young Men**	**Little Children**
Teams of three form Share Groups or Interest Groups to reach unbelievers	Teams of two share the "John 3:16" diagram with those searching for Christ	Values changed; sponsors a new Cell Member and led into ministry

As soon as Little Children or Hurting Persons are ready, they should be trained to share their faith with searching unbelievers. This will help them learn how to reach out, cultivate and care for new persons. At this stage, they are considered Young Men. Each new convert should be bonded into the Cell Group.

Fathers are mature believers who have already led an unbeliever to Christ. They are equipped to create a special group to reach unbelievers who are not seeking for spiritual truth. They form a subgroup sponsored by the rest of the Cell Group. Unlike the weekly Cell Group, this subgroup for developing relationships is short-term, only ten weeks in length. When it is developed around existing relationships with unbelievers, it is called a Share Group. If it is formed for total strangers around a special interest, it is called an Interest Group. These groups are crucial to the penetration and harvesting of unbelievers.

Many unbelievers have become disillusioned about Christians and churches. Unless a special team from the Cell Group develops close relationships with these people, they will remain forever untouched. Since the Cell Group is too intense in its spiritual focus to either attract or hold these persons, the Share Group or Interest Group is essential to reaching them. This team, formed by the Fathers within your Cell Group, will, from time to time, participate in two groups each week: the Cell Group and the group for outreach.

Chapter Ten will further explain these ministries. As a Shepherd, your task is to lead your flock to minister to each other and to the unreached.

CELLS CLUSTER TO FORM CONGREGATIONS

Unlike the "House Church" movement, where each home group is indigenous and independent, Cell Groups relate to each other in a special way. They cluster to form geographical Congregations. It's important to know that the Cell Church uses that word in a new way. In traditional churches the Congregation is the basic building block of the church, and small groups (Cells) are secondary. The word "Congregation" is used by them as a synonym for the word "church." The exact opposite is true in a Cell Church, where the Cells cluster to form many geographical groups, each called a Congregation. A Congregation is an extension of a group of Cell Groups and is formed by them. Congregations don't have a separate life or structure. Instead, "Congregation" defines the activity of Cell Groups uniting for specific tasks.

Sometimes Cells create a congregational worship service. For example, the St. Marys Baptist Church in Sydney, Australia has many Congregations worshipping on Sundays. These are spread over many kilometers. Each Congregation has birthed preachers who

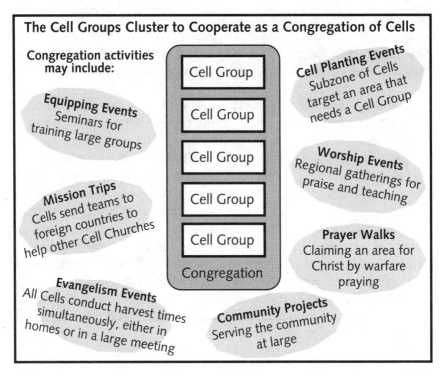

The Cell Groups Cluster to Cooperate as a Congregation of Cells

Congregation activities may include:

Cell Group

Cell Group

Cell Group

Cell Group

Cell Group

Congregation

Equipping Events Seminars for training large groups

Mission Trips Cells send teams to foreign countries to help other Cell Churches

Evangelism Events All Cells conduct harvest times simultaneously, either in homes or in a large meeting

Cell Planting Events Subzone of Cells target an area that needs a Cell Group

Worship Events Regional gatherings for praise and teaching

Prayer Walks Claiming an area for Christ by warfare praying

Community Projects Serving the community at large

meet with the Senior Pastor on Tuesday evenings. Together, they prepare a common sermon which will be delivered in each location the following Sunday. In this way, the Cell Church sponsors small regional worship services which attract local people.

From time to time, the Cell Groups of this church gather for a Celebration service. Hundreds of people gather to worship, pray, study the Bible, and share "dinner on the grounds."

Congregational structures are also used to provide training for Cell members. For example, a Congregation's Cell Leader Interns can be brought together for training. Bible teaching is often done on the Congregational level. Retreats for teens, women, men, etc. can be sponsored by Congregations.

One of the most important tasks of Congregations is to join Cell Groups together for the planting of new Cells. For example, two Congregations of Cells decided to plant new Cells in the unreached area between them.

When several Cells have been established by this joint venturing, a new Subzone is formed. In this manner, new territories are brought under Christ's Lordship.

WHEN SHOULD CONGREGATIONS BE FORMED?

When a Cell Church is being planted, Congregations should be developed when there are five or more Cell Groups in a geographical area. Congregations are most effective when they evolve naturally from the spontaneous fellowship of Cells in geographical areas.

For example, the Yopougon Cell Church in Abidjan, Ivory Coast has many Congregations. As the Cell Groups spread over the city and then into the suburbs, the travel time required to worship in the main sanctuary required their formation.

FIVE OR MORE CONGREGATIONS FORM A ZONE

Each Congregation of five or so Cell Groups will be shepherded by a Zone Supervisor. Congregations then cluster together to form a Zone. A full time Zone Pastor is assigned to the shepherding of this community, which can number 250 people or more.

Usually it is not necessary to form Zones until the Cell Group Church has established twenty to thirty Cell Groups and five or six Congregations (Subzones). If the Cell Groups are healthy and growing, they will double to forty Cells or more in another six to nine months. There will then be a need to form another Zone. As the work grows larger and larger, Zones will form into Districts. A District Pastor will be an overseer of 1,000 or more people in 100 or more Cells comprising 20 Congregations.

District prayer meetings are held approximately every seven weeks in the place of the weekly Cells at Faith Community Baptist Church in Singapore. Their Districts also form special evangelism harvest events and have Leadership Retreats.

As you begin your ministry as a Shepherd, be praying about the future ministry God may have for you. He may well call you to become a Zone Supervisor and then a Zone Pastor!

CELEBRATIONS ASSEMBLE ALL THE CELL GROUPS

Cell Churches vary widely in the way their Celebrations take place. Two basic patterns are frequently seen. The first one is for the Celebration to take place in one location and to be conducted weekly. Faith Community Baptist Church has a two hour weekly

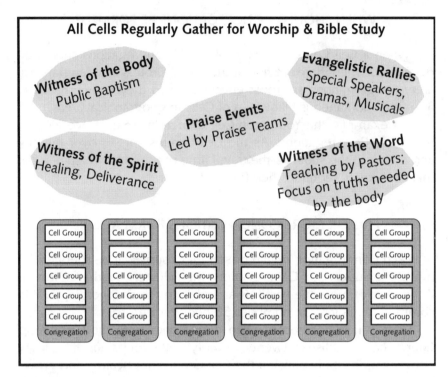

Celebration, repeated four times every Sunday. Each service is attended by as many as 1,600 people. Some of its Cell Groups sit together for the two hour time of worship and Bible teaching. The 12,500 seat Singapore Indoor Stadium is rented periodically for the Sunday Celebration so all the Cell Groups can be together in one location.

A second pattern is for the Congregations to meet weekly and the Celebrations to take place about every six weeks. This is done when the Cells are scattered over wide areas. A classic example of this is DOVE Christian Fellowship, pastored by Larry Kreider. Eleven different Congregations meet in a seven-county area. Some of them meet for Celebrations weekly, while others meet monthly and meet in Cell Groups on Sunday mornings. Larry Kreider states, "Five times since the inception of DOVE we have closed down all of our Sunday morning Celebration meetings at one time and met in homes for approximately a month at a time to strengthen the vision and relationships in the Cells. . . . On one occasion, when we returned back to our Sunday morning Celebrations, we realized that the Lord had added one hundred persons to the church!"

The Yopougon Protestant Baptist Church and Mission in Abidjan, Ivory Coast has only one mass Celebration a year. It is called a "Spiritual Retreat" and is conducted over Easter weekend. In 1986, 9,500 attended. In 1993, over 80,000 attended and 15,000 received Christ.

Cell Churches also use Celebrations for evangelistic outreaches. Faith Community Baptist Church's *Come Celebrate Christmas* event has attracted over 35,000 to its annual presentation. In El Salvador, the Elim Church, pastored by Pastor Sergio Solorzano, has an annual Celebration in an outdoor stadium that draws tens of thousands of people. This Cell Church has 7 Districts, 34 Zone Pastors, 525 Zone Supervisors, and 2,750 Cell Leaders. On Sundays, the seven Celebrations are conducted by Districts. There is a terrible traffic jam between each service as dozens of buses crowd down a two lane road to load and unload thousands of Cell members!

In all cases mentioned, however, the Cells sponsor the Celebration. Instead of the church being built upon a "seeker sensitive service" or some other large meeting attraction, the life of the Body of Christ is in its Cells.

Another important ingredient of a Celebration is solid Bible teaching. Unlike the Program Base Design church, there are no twenty-minute "sermonettes." Typically, the message delivered will be one hour in length. It will seldom be directed toward unbelievers. Instead, it is designed to teach scriptural principles to the Cell members. It is frequently the basis for the edification time in the Cell Groups held during the following week.

YOUR CELL DOES NOT FUNCTION BY ITSELF

Remember, Shepherd, that your flock is not your private "church." Cell Groups are joined together in a vision to reach out to the world beyond. A Cell that does not multiply by winning the lost is not a healthy one. Cancer is a disease caused by Cells that do not properly multiply. You are under the spiritual authority of your Zone Supervisor, your Zone Pastor, your District Pastor, the Senior Pastor and his team. As they pray and strategize about the most effective means of penetrating the darkness of Satan, your Cell is a point of light. A single candle may not be able to light up a large area, but a thousand candles will effectively do so! Your ministry, coupled with all the other Shepherds in your Cell Church, will make a powerful impact!

2

The Qualities of
a Good Shepherd

Shep·herd, noun: A person employed in tending sheep; one who exercises spiritual care over a community; a pastor or minister.

Awesome! You have been assigned by your Lord to "exercise spiritual care over a community!" You are serious about this holy calling, and those in your Cell Group are your assignment.

This manual will help you develop a Shepherd's lifestyle. It will help you create your ministry, and it will provide you with useful tools as you serve.

LET'S LOOK AT YOUR FLOCK . . .

1. It should never have more than fifteen persons attending it.
2. It should begin with five to eight persons.

It's really a "full, part-time job" to care for that many people. If your Shepherd Group becomes larger, you will find yourself unable to care for their needs. Therefore, it's important for you to be committed to multiplying your group as it grows too large for your personalized ministry.

. . . AND YOUR MINISTRY TO THEM.

1. Help each one discover and use their spiritual gifts.
2. Guide each person to have a servant heart, touching others with Christ's love.

You are an enabler, a facilitator. You may or may not be a teacher, a counselor, or an evangelist, but you must always see these tasks within the flock as your primary assignment. As they develop in these two areas, you will touch many areas of life. Sometimes you will be stretched to the limits of your own spiritual capacities, and will seek guidance from your Zone Supervisor. His or her ministry is to meet your needs, prayerfully guiding you to further develop your gifts and enlarge your servant lifestyle.

The family of Christ functions best when each Christian is led by someone who has walked a few steps ahead, and at the same time is caring for others who are a few steps behind. It's a chain of caring. Jesus clearly saw it when He prayed,

> "I have revealed your name to those whom you gave me out of the world. They were yours; you gave them to me and they have obeyed your word. Now they know that everything you have given me comes from you. For I gave them the words you gave me and they accepted them. They knew with certainty that I came from you, and they believed that you sent me. I pray for them . . . All I have is yours, and all you have is mine. And glory has come to me through them. I will remain in the world no longer, but they are still in the world, and I am coming to you. Holy Father, protect them by the power of your name—the name you gave me—so that they may be one as we are one. While I was with them, I protected them and kept them safe by that name you gave me." • John 17:6-12

THE SHEPHERD FOLLOWS HIS LORD'S EXAMPLE

This chain of caring extends all the way from the Father, through the Son, to you. It then extends through you to others. Note Jesus did not say, "I have *taught* your name . . . " Instead, He used the word *revealed.* As a good shepherd, you will be a revealer, not a teacher. Who you are is far more important than what you know.

You will be helped by a personal study of scripture related to shepherding your flock! Using your concordance, look up the word "shepherd" and meditate on the many verses you find. As you read, pray for the Lord to grant you a shepherd's heart.

As a way of explaining to you what your life as a Shepherd should involve, consider the passages that follow. Read each one thoughtfully, thinking about its application to your own life.

A SHEPHERD IS A GUIDE

Moses said to the Lord, "May the Lord, the God of the spirits of all mankind, appoint a man over this community to go out and come in before them, one who will lead them out and bring them in, so the Lord's people will not be like sheep without a shepherd." ·Numbers 27:15-17

This scripture makes it plain there must be two relationships in your life. First, there must be a vertical relationship. You are "a man or woman appointed over this community," responsible to Christ, the Chief Shepherd. Second, there must be a horizontal relationship with your flock. You are responsible for each person:

To the elders among you, I appeal as a fellow elder, a witness of Christ's sufferings and one who also will share in the glory to be revealed: Be shepherds of God's flock that is under your care, serving as overseers—not because you must, but because you are willing, as God wants you to be; not greedy for money, but eager to serve; not lording it over those entrusted to you, but being examples to the flock. And when the Chief Shepherd appears, you will receive the crown of glory that will never fade away. ·1 Peter 5:1-4

A SHEPHERD DOES NOT SEEK SELF-EXALTATION

Consider Jesus' comments about men who took leadership positions to exalt themselves, rather than their God:

Everything they do is done for men to see: They make their phylacteries [That is, boxes containing Scripture verses, worn on forehead and arm] wide and the tassels on their garments long; they love the place of honor at banquets and the most important seats in the synagogues; they love to be greeted in the market places and to have men call them 'Rabbi.' But you are not to be called 'Rabbi,' for you have only one Master and you are all brothers. And do not call anyone on earth 'father,' for you have one Father, and he is in heaven. Nor are you to be called 'teacher,' for you have one Teacher, the Christ. The greatest among you will be your servant. For whoever exalts himself will be humbled, and whoever humbles himself will be exalted. •Matthew 23:5-12

It's pretty clear that being a Shepherd is not for the half-committed! It's a lifestyle of servanthood, isn't it? It involves staying in close contact with your Lord and with your flock. A good Shepherd doesn't ever drive the sheep. Instead, he lovingly leads them.

A SHEPHERD NURTURES

He chose David his servant and took him from the sheep pens; from tending the sheep he brought him to be the shepherd of his people Jacob, of Israel his inheritance. And David shepherded them with integrity of heart; with skillful hands he led them. •Psalm 78:70-72

When they had finished eating, Jesus said to Simon Peter, "Simon son of John, do you truly love me more than these?" "Yes, Lord," he said, "you know that I love you." Jesus said, "Feed my lambs." Again Jesus said, "Simon son of John, do you truly love me?" He answered, "Yes, Lord, you know that I love you." Jesus said, "Take care of my sheep." The third time he said to him, "Simon son of John, do you love me?" Peter was hurt because Jesus asked him the third time, "Do you love me?" He said, "Lord, you know all things; you know that I love you." Jesus said, "Feed my sheep."
•John 21:15-17

Jesus here describes the flock as having lambs and sheep. There is a difference in maturity between those in the flock, and the shepherd recognizes this. The flock is made up of highly individual persons. They cannot be treated as a single entity. Each one has special needs and special capacities.

It is also clear Jesus was not interested in how much wool or meat He could get from His flock, but rather about their needs, and what could be done to serve them. Your reward for your ministry should be Christ's "well done!" That's enough.

Some Christian groups look for "task oriented" personalities, who are then enlisted because they have a particular skill or ability to fill a particular need of the ministry. Thus, more attention is given to finding the "talented" than to others. That should not be true among God's people. You see, without exception, every single Christian is gifted by the Holy Spirit and is expected to exercise spiritual gifts. There is no "hierarchy" among God's people. As we will see, this includes the children in your group.

Satan will strain your understanding of that to the limit. From time to time, your flock will include people who have severely damaged personalities. In most cases, they are passed along unhelped, "unloaded" by one group to another group. As a Shepherd, you will pray over these problemed persons, asking God to enable you to help them become more than they now are. This may require special time with them, or perhaps a loving confrontation about their conduct. We shy away from such people . . . to their detriment.

Nurturing the flock will bring you closer to your Lord than you have ever been before! You will learn to avoid the human tendency to be attracted to the "lovely people" and be condescending to the rest. You will see each person as unique, deeply loved by Christ, with special capacities to minister His life to the redeemed and to the lost alike.

A SHEPHERD PROTECTS

Keep watch over yourselves and all the flock of which the Holy Spirit has made you overseers. Be shepherds of the church of the Lord which he bought with his own blood. I know that after I leave, savage wolves will come in among you and will not spare the flock. Even from your own number men will arise and distort the truth in order to draw away disciples after them. So be on your guard! Remember that for three years I never stopped warning each of you night and day with tears. Now I commit you to God and to the word of his grace, which can build you up and give you an inheritance among all those who are sanctified. •Acts 20:28-32

The word "overseer" in this passage means "to inspect, to look carefully into; a watcher, a guardian." Evaluating all the members of his flock, the Shepherd will ask himself, "What can I do to help this person? What is needed for spiritual growth?" Thus, all members are to be led to greater levels of ministry. Remember always . . . every single member of Christ's body is a minister and is to be guided into the ministry which flows from the spiritual gifts given by God's Spirit!

A SHEPHERD CARES FOR NEEDS

This is what the Sovereign LORD says: Woe to the shepherds of Israel who only take care of themselves! Should not shepherds take care of the flock? You eat the curds, clothe yourselves with the wool and slaughter the choice animals, but you do not take care of the flock. You have not strengthened the weak or healed the sick or bound up the injured. You have not brought back the strays or searched for the lost. You have ruled them harshly and brutally. So they were scattered because there was no shepherd, and when they were scattered they became food for all the wild animals. My sheep wandered over all the mountains and on every high hill . . . As surely as I live, declares the Sovereign LORD, because my flock lacks a shepherd and so has been plundered and has become food for all the wild animals, and because my shepherds did not search for my flock but cared for themselves rather than for my flock, therefore, O shepherds, hear the word of the LORD: . . . I am against the shepherds and will hold them accountable for my flock. I will remove them from tending the flock so that the shepherds can no longer feed themselves. I will rescue my flock from their mouths, and it will no longer be food for them . . . I myself will search for my sheep and look after them. As a shepherd looks after his scattered flock when he is with them, so will I look after my sheep. I will rescue them from all the places where they were scattered on a day of clouds and darkness . . . I will tend them in a good pasture . . . There they will lie down in good grazing land . . . I myself will tend my sheep and have them lie down, declares the Sovereign LORD. I will search for the lost and bring back the strays. I will bind up the injured and strengthen the weak, but the sleek and the strong I will destroy. I will shepherd the flock with justice. •Ezekiel 34:2-16

Note the Lord's references to the "weak and needy." The Shepherd will retrieve rather than abandon, restore rather than reject. Consider this comment, made by a girl who found in a Cell Group a truth that would change her entire life:

"I was divorced in my mid-twenties. I began to charge items in department stores, never considering the dishonesty of buying things I couldn't pay for. Finally, I had created over $11,000 of debt. I got so tired of bill collectors that I moved to another state. Here, I found a Cell Group and began to face my past life for the first time.

"When I openly shared what I had done, some of the men came to my apartment and made me drag out all the bills. Then they had me call every firm and promise them I would begin to make payments to them. At their suggestion, I got a second job, and began to work 16 hours a day, six days a week. I lived on one salary and wrote checks with the other one to repay my debts. Meanwhile, the women in my Cell Group cleaned my apartment, did my laundry, and encouraged me with constant prayer. It took eighteen months to become debt free. I could not meet regularly with the group, but it made no difference. They hovered around me as though they were blood relatives! My Shepherd often dropped in and prayed briefly with me as I worked the second job as a clerk in a discount store.

"I cannot tell you how much I developed spiritually through this experience! For the first time, I realized that every one of us are to minister to others. I was ministered to by our group, and now I have grown in my relationship to

Christ so I can become a minister to others. I will always belong to a Cell Group!"

You will be collecting many stories like this one in the months ahead! Every Shepherd could write a book about the acts of God which takes place in Cell Group sessions. For instance, a couple with a turbulent marriage may discover Christ saying, "Peace! Be still!" through your ministry in the Cell Group. People with terrible self-images will find a new awareness of who they are in Christ. Conversions will occur in a manner that will surprise you. Healings in the areas of the spiritual, emotional, and physical realms will occur, affirming that your Head is actively involved in the life of His body. You will experience the power of Jesus over the demonic as some are delivered from Satan's bondage.

Your prayer life will increase in scope and in power as you continually go to your Lord for wisdom, for power, for direction. In fact, you will agree one year from now, after you have had experience as a Shepherd, that this ministry has brought you closer to Christ than ever before.

A SHEPHERD EQUIPS THE PRIESTS FOR THEIR SERVICE

Peter wrote that every single Christian is a member of Christ's priesthood:

Like newborn babies, crave pure spiritual milk, so that by it you may grow up in your salvation, now that you have tasted that the Lord is good. As you come to him, the living Stone—rejected by men but chosen by God and precious to him—you also, like living stones, are being built into a spiritual house to be a holy priesthood, offering spiritual sacrifices acceptable to God through Jesus Christ . . . But you are a chosen people, a royal priesthood, a holy nation, a people belonging to God, that you may declare the praises of him who called you out of darkness into his wonderful light . . . Live such good lives among the pagans that, though they accuse you of doing wrong, they may see your good deeds and glorify God on the day he visits us.
                                                        •1 Peter 2:2-5, 9, 12

What is the activity of a priest? He stands between a holy God and his fellow man. With one hand he touches God, and with the other hand he touches a person who needs the touch of God! A priest is a channel, and Christ's activity flows through him. That's why Peter says priests must be both "holy" and "royal." The hands which touch God must be *holy* hands; when facing the person with needs, those hands belong to the King, and they are *royal* hands.

Shepherds equip priests to enter their royal service. They are always aware that the sheep are not growing unless they are able to perform priestly service.

Note the term *"being built"* in this passage. Effective priests are not born mature. First, they are "babes" who need milk. Gradually, they mature from one level to another. The word *"being built"* is also translated "edified." Let's stress this fact once again: your ministry as a Shepherd is an equipping ministry, a ministry of building up the believers.

In Ephesians 4:11-13, the ministry of a Shepherd is discussed. Paul points out that the "Gifted Men" are to equip the "Men with Gifts:"

> *It was he who gave some to be apostles, some to be prophets, some to be evangelists, and some to be pastors (shepherds) and teachers, to prepare God's people for works of service, so that the body of Christ may be built up until we all reach unity in the faith and in the knowledge of the Son of God and become mature, attaining to the whole measure of the fullness of Christ.*

The Greek word *poimen* is always translated "shepherd," except for this one verse. (Church tradition alone has caused this different translation to be rendered.) In the early church, every cluster of Christians moving from house to house, breaking bread, fellowshipping, and praying, had a Shepherd. Your ministry is not a modern addition to the church. The office of the *poimen* has existed since the day of Pentecost!

Your job description is to prepare God's people for priestly works of service. Remember that! When you are evaluating your ministry, the questions you will want to ask are, "Have I helped the flock become equipped? Are we as a Cell Group increasing in ministry? Are we building up one another using the spiritual gifts Christ has put in us? Are we influencing unbelievers around us? Are conversions to Christ continual?"

Someone has cynically pointed out that most small groups of Christians become "navel gazing clubs." Insipid, inactive believers who meet to get their own needs met and who ignore their joint ministry to those outside their circle are a blight and a curse to the Kingdom of God! Christ's present body is your flock, and He intends to minister through it. Your calling is not to shelter the flock, but to lead it into ministry. That is why you will be together about six to nine months before you multiply. Never forget that there is another Shepherd in the group: the Holy Spirit. The power of the group is not simply in the development of good group dynamics, but in the active work of the Holy Spirit. It is a humanistic, carnal attitude that causes groups to cling to each other rather than to Jesus, the Head! Veterans of groups that have multiplied regularly have discovered the same dynamic exists in every Cell Group, for the same Lord is Lord of them all. You should see conversions on a regular basis, causing your group to grow to a size where it must multiply to be valid. (Note: groups never "*split*" or "*divide.*" They "*multiply.*")

A SHEPHERD RELIES ON THE HEAD FOR ALL RESOURCES

In Luke 10, Jesus sent out disciples to proclaim Him in the area of Perea. He gave these orders:

> *Go! I am sending you out like lambs among wolves. Do not take a purse or bag or sandals; and do not greet anyone on the road. When you enter a house, first say, 'Peace to this house.' If a man of peace is there, your peace will rest on him; if not, it will return to you. Stay in that house, eating and drinking whatever they give you, for the worker deserves his wages. Do not move around from house to house. When you enter a town and are welcomed, eat what is set before you. Heal the sick who are there and tell them, 'The kingdom of God is near you.'* •Luke 10:3-9

Several surprising things leap out of this passage. First, He must have scared them to death when He told them they would be "like lambs among wolves." Lambs must always trust the Shepherd for protection.

Second, they were not to "greet anyone on the road." Their assignment was top priority and came before personal interests. Becoming a part of the Kingdom is like joining an army. You simply don't have a conflict of priorities where battles are concerned. As one Australian said, "A Christian must be flat out for God."

Third, they were not to take extra money or other items of clothing with them. Thus, they would have to trust in God to provide both for their own needs and for the needs of those they met. They would not become "fund raisers," but would expect their Master to provide power for the encounters they would face. The issues were spiritual, not physical. (After all, they were entering warfare against Satan!) Neither money, shirts, or sandals would suffice for those who needed inner peace and deliverance!

What Christ wants us to offer people is Himself. He alone is adequate for men's needs. We must never settle for giving others anything less than Christ, flowing from our lives to transform the lives of others.

As we discover the flow of Christ's powerful life through us, we learn we cannot minister solely through welfare gifts, psychological evaluations, and Bible studies for the sake of studying the Bible. Bringing "good news to the poor" is not accomplished by presenting people with keys to a new car. Bringing "freedom for the prisoners" is not done with bail bond money. Causing "recovery of sight for the blind" is not achieved by providing a hospitalization policy. "Releasing the oppressed" is not achieved through prescribing tranquilizers. When the Priest is fully equipped, he or she will know how to bring a broken life or relationship to Christ. His power alone can release people from the bondage of the evil one.

Shepherd, you cannot ever lead others where you have not walked. How is your prayer life? How steadily do you rely on Christ for your own needs? How often do you cast yourself before Him, discovering He is adequate for your own situation? How many times have you messed up your life, only to watch in astonishment as His love remained unchanged toward you? From these personal experiences, you will lead others to travel where you have walked.

SAY "GOODBYE" TO YOUR OLD LIFESTYLE

It's obvious, isn't it, that being a Shepherd means a new way of viewing life. The Shepherd never says, "I will tend the flock on Wednesday evenings from 7:00 to 9:30 p.m." No! The Shepherd lives with the flock, sleeps in the fields with the flock, goes into treacherous situations to find a lost sheep, and carries the lambs in his arms. The Shepherd is the first one to go into the "valley of the shadow of death" to lead sheep to "green pastures."

Obviously, this is not a calling for people with butterfly personalities, who are going to flit from flower to flower as their whims dictate. Reading through 1 Timothy will help you recognize that what a Shepherd does is barely mentioned. The focus is on a Shepherd's character and lifestyle.

The best thing you can do to prepare yourself for your ministry as a Shepherd is to come to the cliff edge of your own capacities and throw yourself over—knowing that if Christ's adequacy is not there for you, you are in serious trouble! Let's begin! Confessing your inadequacy, jump!

3

The Shepherd as
an Equipper

DISCIPLING IS A CHAIN OF CARING AND SHARING

Jesus' commission to us is found in Matthew 28:18-20:

Then Jesus came to them and said, "All authority in heaven and on earth has been given to me. Therefore go and make disciples of all nations, baptizing them into the name of the Father and of the Son and of the Holy Spirit, and teaching them to obey everything I have commanded you. And surely I am with you always, to the very end of the age."

What does it mean to "make disciples?" The Greek here is *matheteusate,* a word that requires forty-four pages to explain in the *Theological Dictionary of the New Testament!* These points will help us to understand the diagram on page 37:

1. The one being equipped depends on the equipper.
2. Basic to the whole relationship is the inner fellowship between the two, and the practical effects of it.
3. The relationship is not merely an external connection with the goal of picking up information or skills under expert direction.

4. It is grounded in a fellowship which arises because all who participate are equally striving.

Martin Luther once said, "The simplest peasant, armed with the Gospel, is mightier than the Pope!" We must permit every Christian to exercise the biblical right to minister to others. In 1 Corinthians 14:26, Paul makes it plain that everyone is to be involved in building up others. A part of spiritual growth requires me to become responsible for someone else. If that is not taking place, my maturity as a Christian will be stunted.

Have you ever had the experience of learning something for yourself, and then having to teach it? If you have, you know how much you profited by passing it on. When you pass on what you know, you enter a new plateau of maturity. The act of being taught by someone else, learning for yourself, and passing it on to someone, is the correct biblical pattern for discipleship. Most people grow and change by watching others, not just by reading books.

No two of us are at the same milestone in our Christian journey. Ages, temperaments, and needs make each group unique. In the months to come, you will discover this for yourself as your Cell Group grows and multiplies: your second group will be as different from your first one as a firstborn son is from his little brother!

Consider the three levels in the Cell Group as seen by John:

I write to you, dear children, because your sins have been forgiven on account of his name. I write to you, fathers, because you have known him who is from the beginning. I write to you, young men, because you have overcome the evil one. I write to you, dear children, because you have known the Father. I write to you, fathers, because you have known him who is from the beginning. I write to you, young men, because you are strong, and the word of God lives in you, and you have overcome the evil one. •1 John 2:12-14

It's important to have a proper mixture of the levels of spiritual maturity when forming groups. To be an effective community, there should be "children," "young men," (of course, the terms refer to both women and men!) and "fathers." Note the levels of spiritual maturity in these three groups:

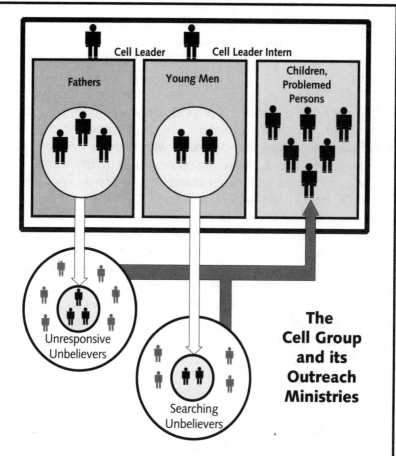

The Cell Group and its Outreach Ministries

This illustration shows a Cell Group at the multiplication stage. The members have reached out in two ways. The YOUNG MEN have been contacting people who are responsive to the Gospel. The FATHERS have been relating to the unresponsive through Share Groups or Interest Groups.

The converts, along with Christians who need spiritual or emotional healing, are in the first subgroup. They are being nurtured by the YOUNG MEN and the FATHERS. Gradually they will move into the YOUNG MEN group.

Usually the Cell Leader Intern focuses on ministry to the problemed persons, since they need a lot of attention. As the Cell Leader, you will be concentrating on the outreach ministry of the group and guiding the equipping processes.

LEVEL ONE: The Children know forgiveness of sins, and know the Father . . . not with the deeper knowledge the fathers have of Him, but with a simple, childlike trust. These are represented by the first level in the diagram: New Believers and Problemed Persons.

LEVEL TWO: The Young Men have overcome the evil one by their knowledge of the word of God. They are no longer tricked by the lies and accusations of Satan, who is described as the "accuser of the brethren." They can do battle with experienced eyes, knowing how he will attack. These are represented by the second level in the diagram: teams who reach searching, responsive people.

LEVEL THREE: The Fathers truly know God and function knowing whatever is bound in heaven can be bound on earth. As a husband knows the thoughts and desires of his wife after twenty years of marriage, even so spiritual "Fathers" know God's ways intimately. These are represented by the highest levels in the diagram: the Fathers, the Cell Leader, and the Cell Leader Intern.

These divisions, or levels, shown in this diagram are artificially inserted. They are only used to help you recognize the levels of spiritual maturity suggested for effective discipleship to take place.

This structure is based on the conviction that every person needs someone to help spiritual growth occur. Equipping disciples is not the assignment of a few "super-Christians," but must be the activity of all Christians.

At the beginning of the chain of people-equipping-people is the brand new Christian. These newborns are to be treated as babes who *"crave pure spiritual milk, so that by it (they) may grow up in (their) salvation."* Beginning with them, a chain of caring for one another is established. One who has walked a few steps ahead of someone else can share what has already been learned, and the journeys continue. Thus, a "Sponsor-Sponsee" structure must be established in your Cell Group.

THE FIRST LEVEL: WORKING WITH NEW CHRISTIANS AND PROBLEMED PERSONS

The first level in the Cell Group includes new believers and problemed persons. Neither type can effectively become involved in ministry until after they are nurtured and matured.

Assign each new believer in the group to a Sponsor—one who will help this person become established in his/her walk with Christ. *The Arrival Kit* has been written to help this take place. Over a period of eleven weeks, a new believer can usually mature enough to move into the middle division.

Problemed persons need the nurture of the entire group, but should be specially cared for by you and your Servant Intern. One type will be going through a temporary period of crisis, such as the death of a loved one, a divorce, loss of employment, etc. Like someone who has influenza, these persons must be temporarily helped until recovery takes place. They can then move into the middle level.

Another type of hurting person is the *chronically problemed* person. These individuals are often tolerated in a Cell Group until it is time for them to be passed on at multiplication time. Some are limited by their personality structure. Others never get out of their syndrome simply because people avoid them. Their personalities are often anti-social. Sometimes they constantly say tactless things. In a later chapter, we will consider how they can be helped.

THE SECOND LEVEL: WORKING WITH "TYPE A" PEOPLE

Develop Young Men at the second level by giving them experience. One characteristic of being immature is impatience. When children want something, they are not able to wait. They want it— now! This is also true with younger Christians who have not yet learned how to wage war against the attacks of Satan. It is best to assign a ministry to this believer which will produce quick results.

For this reason, many Cell Churches assign their Cell Groups to counseling "Type A" unbelievers who accept Christ at the close of Celebration services. This is a perfect opportunity for a Young Man to experience the joy of helping someone accept Christ.

As a Cell Leader, assign the Young Men to work in teams of two. They should visit with responsive unbelievers who are open to the Gospel. These names have been passed on to your Cell Group for further contact and ministry, perhaps because of age, geographical location, etc. They need to be brought to Christ and included in your group.

What could be a better starting place than visiting someone who wants to be visited? These contacts provide experience in meeting people, sharing in their needs, and inviting them to become a part of your Cell Group. If they are not yet Christians, it is usually because no one has explained how they can receive Christ as Lord and Savior.

This is a task for the Young Men. As the illustration on page 37 suggests, they bring these new believers into your Cell Group and sponsor them. In doing so, new ministry experiences are added to their lives.

A diagram based on John 3:16, taught in the *Touching Hearts Guidebook*, equips those who will participate in this ministry. The material expects the one being discipled to actually make visits with "Type A" unbelievers. Thus, it provides "on the job training" for those who are doing this for the first time.

THE THIRD LEVEL: WORKING WITH "TYPE B" PEOPLE

Develop Fathers by involving them with the hard to reach. The "Type B" unbelievers are not searching for Jesus Christ and show no

"Type A"   "Type B"

Your Cell Group will multiply as your members reach out to two types of unbelievers. "Type A" is a term used to describe those who are searching for peace with God. "Type B" are those who are so preoccupied with life and its challenges and problems that they have ignored their spiritual needs. The first can be quickly reached. The second group will require prayer and patience as they are cultivated and exposed to the life of your Cell members.

interest in Bible study or other Christian activities. Only mature Christians can reach them. Like a mother pregnant with child, this "special forces" team must carry the burden of Type B unbelievers for many months before seeing them born again. Deliverance may be required as well.

This outreach is achieved by forming a second small group usually called a Share Group or an Interest Group. As shown on page 37, this short-term group meets separately from the Cell Group. For periods of ten weeks, probably once each year, these mature Christians will have two group meetings to attend: their Cell Group and their Share or Interest Group. Each week, this Share Group team will move from house to house, relating to "Type B" unbelievers in discussing topics that are non-religious. At the same time, in private they will be probing for new responsiveness to spiritual matters.

The commitment of time required to meet with both the Cell Group and the Share/Interest Group is significant. Only mature Christians who have "put away lesser things" will devote themselves to this dedicated lifestyle.

Experience has shown that once a Christian has entered into a Share/Interest Group ministry, they rapidly mature in the Lord. They will be thrust into new levels of faith which make possible God's further calling for them to consider becoming a Shepherd.

Special guidebooks have been written to equip these "green berets" of God's army. The team conducts a Share/Interest Group during their equipping times. Five days of daily devotionals reinforce the experiences provided in the Share/Interest Groups. On-the-job training guarantees maximum effectiveness.

AGAIN . . . SAY "GOODBYE" TO YOUR OLD LIFESTYLE!

If you have a history of working in or belonging to a traditional church, you probably suffer from the curse of a compartmentalized lifestyle. You have pigeonholed your activities: there is "work life," "home life," "recreational life," "leisure life," etc. Like a mailman who sorts out letters and tosses them into different bins, you have spent your life throwing bits of time into different bins.

The problem with that is that time is not your property, and you have no right to toss it around. The Lordship of Jesus Christ is never more real than where your time is concerned! If you are submitted to Him as a Servant, He will totally possess your time. If you are in perfect fellowship with Him, you can trust Him to give you exactly the time you need for all that is really important in your life. Being a Shepherd will not rob you of your ministry to your own family, for they are a vital part of it. So is your testimony in the "market place" where you are employed. God knows how much relaxation time you need, and you can trust Him to also give it to you.

You will be very frustrated if you try to be in charge of your life's time frame and simultaneously let Christ be in charge of your ministry activity. If you will totally, completely yield all your time to Him, He will give you peace within and time to do what is really important. He may loose you from the bondage of too many commitments, helping you to see the time traps Satan has used to keep you exhausted. He will cause you to become a Mary, with time to sit at His feet, rather than a Martha, who busied herself with all the preparations she thought had to be made.

Erase from your mind forever the idea that the work of being a Shepherd will take one night or morning a week. It's a lifestyle. It's your life's style! The Shepherd's care is based on pure love for Christ and for the sheep. Paul's shepherd heart caused him to see the flock as his "*dear children, for whom I am again in the pains of childbirth until Christ is formed in you . . .* " (Galatians 4:19). You will discover the Lord will allow you to fit in all the needed time to minister, but there will certainly be no "ordered pattern" to it. Like firemen, who are always ready to go to a fire, you will learn to be prepared for the moments when it is impossible to say, "I am too busy to care for you just now." At the same time, you will discover that for every "yes" in your life there will be four or five "no's" required. The time you spend alone with your Lord in prayer will be the most important of all. As you complete this chapter, take some time to pray. Reflect again on the various spiritual levels of the people you care for, and seek His leadership of your life as you equip them.

Part Two

The
Shepherd's
Tasks

4

As You Go,
Develop Apprentices

In all probability, in about six to nine months your Cell Group will have grown to fifteen members, and it will be necessary to multiply it into two Cells. At that time, your Servant Intern must be capable of shepherding half the group. From the very first week you are together, concentrate on equipping your associate to be ready for this time.

The pattern for this is found in 2 Timothy 2:2:

And the things you have heard me say in the presence of many witnesses entrust to reliable men who will also be qualified to teach others.

Consider the pattern of sharing which is described by Paul. His equipping was seldom, if ever, done using a "one on one" pattern. He refers to the "many witnesses" who observed the way he worked with Timothy. Both Jesus and Paul discipled men in small groups, rather than doing it in private. Follow their example by equipping your Intern before the observing Cell Group. This will provide the members with an example to follow as they themselves serve as Sponsors. Even though what you are doing with your Intern is not mentioned by them, the impact made by watching you will be real.

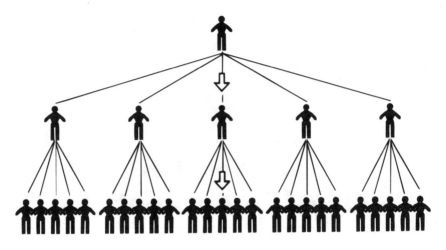

Paul was anxious for Timothy to learn how to equip others. Note his reference to reliable people. Evaluating those who are to be trained is an important part of the discipling process. Teach your Intern how to determine each team member's readiness for ministry by evaluating him or her.

Timothy's task was not only to pass on what Paul taught him, but to also pass on the method of equipping others. As Paul monitored Timothy, so Timothy would learn to watch those he had taught. He had to be sure the discipleship pattern could be recycled down to the third generation.

The most ineffective way of developing your Servant Intern is by using one of the many discipleship courses available. Christianity is saturated with notebooks, study guides, and lesson plans. Those who have spent months using this pattern of discipleship usually end up having good devotions, but few people have actually developed the capacity to shepherd others. The reason is obvious: shepherding is not taught; it's caught. That's why Paul wrote,

> . . . our gospel came to you not simply with words, but also with power, with the Holy Spirit and with deep conviction. You know how we lived among you for your sake. You became imitators of us and of the Lord; in spite of severe suffering, you welcomed the message with the joy given by the Holy Spirit. And so you became a model to all the believers in Macedonia and Achaia . . . •1 Thessalonians 1:5-7

Norman Coad, missionary to Africa, has written, "In apprenticeship, a young person will live and work alongside a master craftsman for years until the necessary skills are developed. It, therefore, seems proper that some form of apprenticeship education should be used to propagate the Gospel."

Right on, Norman! We have made enough "Bible-worms" through our bookish discipleship techniques. A more New Testament way of equipping disciples is to develop apprentices.

Moses trained Joshua as an apprentice. Elijah had a School of the Prophets, but none of them developed as did Elisha, the apprentice. John the Baptist's apprentices followed him around, as did Jesus' disciples. Apprenticeship is the Bible way of developing your Intern.

For example, a sharp young man named Fred came to me and said, "Would you be willing to disciple me?" He had already become active in a Share Group ministry, and had strong potential for serving as a Cell Leader or even a Pastor in future years. I prayed about the time I would have to invest before I gave him an answer. When the Lord told me to proceed, I said, "Fred, I'll meet with you every Wednesday night for a while, and we'll spend other times of the week together as the Lord directs."

"Great!" he said; "Shall I come to your office?"

"No," I replied. "Where's the closest tavern to your house?"

Fred looked at me in amazement. "I don't know."

"Well, drive around your neighborhood and find it. Give me the address, and I'll meet you there next Wednesday night at seven." Fred had his first equipping session with me in a tavern. He learned how I met pagan men and shared my faith with them in a relational, no push-no shove way. Then I watched as he learned to do the same thing in bars. I saw boldness develop in him.

In the following weeks, Fred went with me as I ministered to an ex-con who was ready to commit suicide. Such events were to be Fred's training ground. Soon after, a phone call came to us from a man who had a .45 automatic on his lap, ready to take his life because his wife had left him. As I talked, Fred traced the call. We drove frantically to his home and ministered to him face to face. Fred ended up hiring the man to work in his business, counseling and witnessing daily with him. The apprentice had an apprentice! He spent many hours developing his ability to minister by discipling that man.

As the months wore on, I intentionally saw Fred less and less. (This is the stage called "benign neglect.") He no longer required me to tell him what to do. I began to pray with him about ministry problems he was facing. I was not surprised when he told me he was going to Moscow with a witnessing team for a few weeks. When he returned, we spent several hours together, rejoicing in the reports of God's power manifested as he went underground with some really tough Moscow youths.

I was not surprised when Fred called to tell me he was selling his landscape business and was going to attend seminary in preparation for further Christian service.

Using the same pattern, your Shepherd Intern needs to be involved in all you do during the six months you will be together. Planning group meetings, visiting the lost, dropping in on Share or Interest Groups, counselling stressed-out persons, praying for the sheep—all these should be done together.

Here's the pattern for apprenticing:

1. Your Intern watches you.
2. You explain what you did and why you did it.
3. You observe as your apprentice does the same thing.
4. You encourage and objectively explain strengths and weaknesses you've observed.
5. You provide remedial activity to strengthen the weaknesses.
6. You turn the task over to the Intern.
7. You withdraw, using "benign neglect" as your strategy.
8. You closely monitor as your apprentice disciples a new Intern.
9. You remain a close friend, now treating your Intern as your equal.

Your Intern will graduate from being a beginner to one developing as a servant person, to becoming a mature Shepherd. Or, to put it as John did, he or she will move from the category of Children to Young Men to Fathers.

Tips for teaching your Intern to lead Cell Group sessions:

1. Discuss in advance what you are going to do in each meeting, and explain why you are taking such an approach.
2. After each Cell Group, discuss what you have both learned from the meeting. Then, plan the next one together.

3. Discuss problems, such as a person who caused the group to get bogged down by overtalking. Take your Intern with you everywhere you serve!
4. As you discern your Intern is ready for the experience, turn the group sessions over to him or her.
5. Evaluate the strengths and weaknesses which are revealed as the meeting is facilitated. Frankly discuss your conclusions. Assign remedial tasks to help weak ministry skills further develop.
6. Turn the ministry of the Cell Group over to your Intern during the final month before multiplication time. By following this process, flock members will have confidence in their new Shepherd when two groups are formed from the one.

Tips for ministering to the members of the flock with your Intern:

1. Take your Intern along every time you have a *Journey Guide* interview, reviewing the results together.
2. On appropriate occasions, let the Intern sit in on counseling sessions. Afterwards, discuss why you did what you did.
3. Let the Intern accompany you when making visits and contacts.
4. Let the Intern observe you winning others to Christ.
5. Go on an overnight prayer retreat together, and really pray!

Finally, stay close to your Intern after the daughter group is launched. Monitor closely the pattern being used to develop a new Intern. Be open about deficiencies you see. Don't ignore your Intern during this crucial period, even though "benign neglect" is now your new pattern.

FORMS ARE ON PAGES 245 AND 246 FOR
EVALUATING YOUR INTERN . . . AND ALSO ONE FOR YOU!

5

Equipping the
Flock for Ministry

Shepherd, you are the only person directly responsible for the spiritual growth of your flock! You cannot take this matter too seriously. In *Go And Make Apprentices*, Philip Vogel writes:

> God's aim for the believer is maturity, and the provision He has made of gifts and ministries are for that end. They are given to prepare and repair (literally meaning to mend the nets) God's people for works of service so that the body may be built up and attain that goal of maturity (Eph. 4:11-16). Just as it is the responsibility of every parent to prepare and guide their children towards maturity, so it is the responsibility of Christian leaders to disciple believers towards maturity.

HOW DO YOU MEASURE SPIRITUAL GROWTH?

Measuring maturity is tricky! I have two grandchildren who live in California. We get to see them two or three times a year. When they come bouncing into the house, the first sign of change we observe is their physical growth. Grandma says, "Ruthie! You have grown three inches!" Little Ruthie beams with pride—as though she had personally triumphed over being smaller! We notice she no longer throws food on the floor. Mother lets her feed herself. She asks to go to the bathroom. Marvelous!

After a few hours with my grandson, I think: "Nathan's vocabulary has grown. He's writing new words, and he's also learning new facts. His little mind has grown."

At the close of a meal my son says to them, "Let's recite our scripture verses for Maw Maw and Paw Paw." I listen as they speak the memorized words, rejoicing that spiritual foundations have been laid within them.

Then they get tired. Ruthie screams like a Banshee Indian when Nathan takes her favorite toy. He changes his cherubic facial expression, and glares with selfishness. She throws another toy at him. Oh, dear! They are, indeed, still immature babies. I take Nathan to my office and say, "Nathan, you are a big boy now. Why do you still steal Ruthie's toys? You are too old to act like that." He looks at me in stony silence. My mature words are not in his childish vocabulary; I am wasting my breath on him. Sadly, I realize such conversations between us are years away . . .

How do we measure maturity in these children? By knowing where they were, by seeing where they are, and by discerning where they must develop. You will use these same guidelines with those in your flock. Where have they been? Are they responsible for their own lives, or are they controlled by circumstances? Do they know who they are in God? Do the decisions and choices they make reveal a God-centered value system? Are their jokes reflecting carnal allusions to sexuality? Do they pray "on command," not at all, or with an appetite for fellowship with the Father?

Later in this book you will be introduced to the *Journey Guide*. It is necessary for you to get to know each incoming Cell member in a personal way. This is designed to help you do so. You will note that one of the queries asks for the names of two people who have been used as a pattern for his or her lifestyle (page 10 in the *Journey Guide*). These are special people who have had great influence in the past in this person's life. Their values have been adopted and reproduced. If you can personally meet these two people, do so. Knowing those who have impacted this Cell member's life is a key to your future ministry to him or her.

BEING MATURE IS MEASURED BY
HOW COMMITTED WE ARE

The extent of a person's spiritual maturity is the extent of the commitment he or she has to Kingdom activity. This way of measuring maturity is most important. Your assignment can be reduced to one simple statement: Encourage your flock members to be totally responsible for properly exercising their spiritual gifts.

Traditional church life robs the believer of being responsible. The pastor does all the Bible study for the congregation and shares his findings in the auditorium. The Christian is never exposed to biblical content in its entirety, never encouraged to purchase a basic set of books for personal research and study. When the believer has problems, he is given advice about what to do. If he has an illness, someone comes to pray at the hospital bedside. If a friend needs to accept Jesus, an appointment is made for him with the pastor.

Ninety per cent of the contributions come from ten percent of the members. This ten per cent also holds ninety per cent of the church offices. Church rolls are shambled by fifty per cent or more being listed as "inactive." While the typical pastor works seventy hours a week, the church members complain if they have to attend six hours of activities a week. For them, being a Christian is not a lifestyle; it's a category, often seconded to other categories like work, school and family time.

Shepherd, your task is to bring responsibility into its biblical framework for each member of your flock. Help your Cell Group naturally manifest their spiritual gifts to build up one another. Consider this scripture:

What then shall we say, brothers? When you come together, everyone has a hymn, or a word of instruction, a revelation, a tongue or an interpretation. All of these must be done for the strengthening of the church. •*1 Corinthians 14:26*

Everyone! Everyone! Everyone! No exceptions! All participate!

Do you know what your biggest handicap will be as you begin your ministry as a Shepherd? Over control and over protectiveness of the flock. You can hold back the work of the Holy Spirit by not creating opportunities for them to discover and use their spiritual gifts. You will find most people are able to exercise them much sooner than expected. By letting the gifts flow at each person's level of maturity, the members of the group model their use before the others.

Helping your Cell members develop their spiritual gifts is a process. If the proper environment is provided, maturity will result. If the group is encouraged to hear God's voice and respond by ministering to one another, edification will take place in a natural way.

Many people feel they cannot exercise a spiritual gift unless they are "zapped" by the Holy Spirit. The weeks go by, and they continually await a "glorious feeling" that will assure them that God is working through them. The emotional bubble bath they are waiting for, which they think is necessary before they will receive spiritual gifts, never comes. Thus, they are robbed of their ministries.

Since Christians do not go into trance-like states which produce spiritual gifts, the work of the Holy Spirit will always be accomplished by our deliberate cooperation with Him. We must cooperate with the Spirit of God by entering into ministry. As a Cell Leader, you have the perfect climate to call forth the gifts of your flock. As needs are shared, gifts will flow. Model for the group how this takes place.

As I face a need in the life of another person, the gifts of the Holy Spirit will flow through me. Encourage the group to edify one another. Explain that our capacities to build up each other are caused by the indwelling Holy Spirit, and ministering to one another is the way to discover our gifts.

You might also explain this scripture to the Cell group:

Two or three prophets should speak, and the others should weigh carefully what is said. •1 Corinthians 14:29

The term "prophet" used in this chapter would seem to be used in two ways. First, there is the specific gift of prophecy. There seems to also be a general use of the term by Paul to refer to any of the gifts of the Holy Spirit. They include "intelligible words to instruct" (verse 19), and may involve any gift that edifies the group.

The point made by this verse is simply that "the others should weigh carefully what is said." Who are the "others?" One Bible teacher with a P.B.D. mind-set has suggested it refers to the "Elders of the church." That is patently nonsense. The elders could not be present in every Cell Group, and the activities described in this chapter could only take place if the group is small enough for everyone to exercise spiritual gifts (see verse 26). Therefore, the "others" must refer to the Cell Group members themselves. It is in the continual evaluation of the use of the gifts by the entire group that they learn how to discern what is from God and what is not.

Consider this taking place in your Cell Group: A young Christian gives a "word of knowledge" in the meeting. As you listen to it, you know that the remark contradicts Scripture. What should you do? Should you courteously ignore the word given? No! Use the moment to help the Cell Group "weigh carefully what is said." You might say, "Our little sister in the Lord is seeking to know the difference between her own thoughts and the thoughts the Lord is giving. As we think of her words to us, can we help her know if this came from the Lord, or was it her own impression?" In the discussion which would follow, the proper scripture references could be quoted to indicate the word is not in keeping with biblical truth. An encouraging comment can then be spoken by you: "Sister, we are all proud of you. You are seeking to know the voice of the Lord so you may edify others. We want to encourage you to continue with your prayer life. As your times in the Listening Room increase, you will be able to know more clearly the word of the Lord given to you to build up others." Consider the impact upon the entire Cell Group from such experiences!

CREATE THE RIGHT ENVIRONMENTS FOR GROWTH

1. The Directive Environment

Simply stated, this is the "Tell and Show" environment. First, you explain to a member of the Cell Group what it means to receive a direction from the Lord to build up another believer. Next, you personally model what you have explained. Following this, you create Sponsor-Sponsee connections between the members, beginning with the new converts. Edification will take place as often in these Sponsor-Sponsee contacts as in the actual Cell Group.

This environment for growth must also include your modeling how to reach out to unbelievers with the Gospel. Lead the group

The Right Environments for Equipping

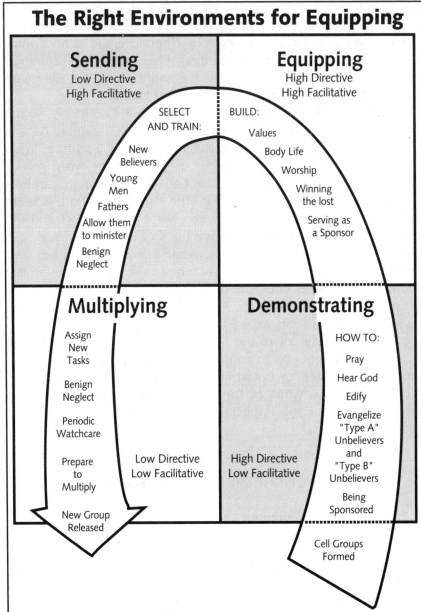

Sending
Low Directive
High Facilitative

SELECT
AND TRAIN:

New
Believers

Young
Men

Fathers

Allow them
to minister

Benign
Neglect

Equipping
High Directive
High Facilitative

BUILD:

Values

Body Life

Worship

Winning
the lost

Serving as
a Sponsor

Multiplying

Assign
New
Tasks

Benign
Neglect

Periodic
Watchcare

Prepare
to
Multiply

New Group
Released

Low Directive
Low Facilitative

Demonstrating

HOW TO:

Pray

Hear God

Edify

Evangelize
"Type A"
Unbelievers
and
"Type B"
Unbelievers

Being
Sponsored

High Directive
Low Facilitative

Cell Groups
Formed

In the six to nine months you will shepherd your group, it is possible to take each person through the cycle shown above. The experiences they will share in the weekly Cell Groups and in ministry to unbelievers will cause the use of spiritual gifts to develop.

into the evangelizing of "Type A" and "Type B" unbelievers by form-ing Visitation Teams and a Share Group or an Interest Group.

Of course, a few of your sheep will be unable to move at the same pace as the majority. They may be burning up all their ener-gies trying to survive in a stressed-out life and need to be the receivers of edification. You will lovingly help them in the same directive way, but toward the goal of becoming whole persons. You will minister to them. You will model for them your own lifestyle of walking by faith, not fear. Encourage them to take "baby steps," becoming responsible for themselves. Frankly evaluate their progress. When they become healthy once again, the sign of this progress will be their ability to care about and minister to others. Helping the Cell members edify and evangelize is made much easier by the modeling of peers in the group who are actively reaching out. It is contagious to be surrounded by excited Christians who are actively ministering to others.

2. The Facilitative Environment

This may be called the "Send and Encourage" environment. The members are involved in the equipping modules, learning either to adopt Kingdom values, to share the "John 3:16" presentation, or to establish Share/Interest Group relationships. You may decide to actually help these Christians launch their ministries by participating with them for a couple of weeks.

Gradually, your Cell Group time will include "Share the Vision" reports from ministry activities and you will conduct seasons of prayer for the spiritual problems being confronted. Your group meetings will focus on the value systems of the members. Worship and Body Life will become richer and richer. New people will be added to the group as a result of the ministry activities and you will busy yourself with incorporating them as new family members.

Meditate on the mingling of the two environments, noting the shifts in their use in the four stages of Demonstrating, Equipping, Sending and Multiplying. Discuss them with your Apprentice.

Later in this book you will find a number of Cell Group meetings outlined for you. Notice how they progress through these stages. Use the series at least once, learning through them to function as a Facilitator.

DEALING WITH STRONGHOLDS

The weapons we fight with are not the weapons of the world. On the contrary, they have divine power to demolish strongholds. We demolish arguments and every pretension that sets itself up against the knowledge of God and we take captive every thought to make it obedient to Christ.
                                        •2 Corinthians 10:4-5

The word for "stronghold" used in this passage describes a well established, strongly defended fortress. It guards the entrance to a territory or a trade route. For example, Jericho and Ai were strongholds which had to be overcome by the Israelites.

Wherever strongholds are ignored, Satan controls. God told Israel to utterly destroy all strongholds in the land. Their unwillingness to do so caused them endless misery and finally the downfall of their nation. You will face Satan's strongholds in the lives of your flock. Your best means of learning how to deal with them is to first attack strongholds in your own life.

Strongholds are the enemies of growth. With your Intern, you will be spending time with individual members who need to be set free. These times are crucial to the deliverance of Christians who have spent years struggling in the swamps of self-doubt and shame.

When Mary (not her real name) entered my office, she was using an aluminum walker to support herself. At the age of thirty-six, she already had a ten year history of back operations, physical therapy, medications and even psychotherapy for spinal problems. Her parents had spent thousands of dollars trying to help her!

"Mary," I said, "I am not a physician. Yet, you have come to me with your back problem. I can only discern that in your life there are spiritual reasons for your visit. Tell me—is there a stronghold of sin in your life which is causing your pain?"

Mary began to share a story of adultery with a married man in her mid-twenties. After a year, he threw her away like a used facial tissue. From a fine Christian home, Mary had violated all her own morals by yielding to his advances. She moved back home. It was then her back problems began.

"Mary, have you asked God to forgive you? Has He done so?"

"Oh, yes! I prayed for forgiveness years ago. I know He has forgiven me."

I asked, "But have you forgiven yourself?"

Eyes filled with tears as she replied, "I can't! What I did was too awful! I can't forgive myself."

"Mary, don't you realize there is a greater sin than adultery in your life? You have set up your self-judgment seat higher than God's and have found yourself guilty by a court higher than His. You have created a life sentence for yourself, punishing yourself unconsciously by this back ailment. You have a stronghold of unbelief. You have rejected the grace and mercy and forgiveness of God in your heart. Is not that the source of your illness?"

She thought for a long time and then slowly replied, "You are right. I guess I have known it all along. I have become higher than God in judging my sin."

I explained that she herself had to pray, confessing her sin and asking God to cast out the stronghold which had made her suffer pain for years. I stood and placed my hands on her head and she sobbed out her words to her Master. As I prayed, the Father gave me full assurance that she was delivered—fully released—and would never have back problems again. When I finished praying, I took her by the hand and said, "Mary, let's go for a walk."

She looked at me with surprise and then reached for her stroller. I kicked it across the room. "You will never use it again. Let's go for a walk!" Slowly, she rose to her feet. A look of joy flooded over her as we began to walk toward the door of my office. Fifty feet later, we actually danced a little jig together! Mary was delivered from Satan's stronghold in her life and for several years has lived in the newness of a healed life.

Don't be afraid to bring the great power of God against the puny holds Satan places in the lives of those you will serve. He is the Great Deliverer and "nothing, nothing—absolutely nothing—nothing is too difficult for God!"

6

The "Year of Equipping"

An older generation sang, "Onward, Christian Soldiers, Marching As To War." Our generation has created a similar song: "God's got an army, marching through the land." If we dare to take either of these songs literally, a Cell Church must define itself as a task-oriented community, storming Hell's gates, snatching broken lives from Satan's grip.

In the Cell Church, every member shares a common vision: a Cell of seven or eight people, challenged to multiply to 14 or 15 in a period of six to nine months. All Cell members are ministers, reaching out to bring the lost to Jesus Christ—and that means face-to-face contact with the unreached. New Christians and transfers from other churches must be prepared for such a lifestyle.

In an army, recruits are sent through a rigorous basic training course. Bodies are toughened and minds are disciplined. Warfare skills are rehearsed. Battle-hardened men are assigned to teach novices. When soldiers go into battle, they can depend on each other because of the special training they have been given.

Likewise, those who are trained for spiritual warfare must be fully prepared when placed in ministry situations. Cell members must be able to reach unbelievers with the message of Christ's love. As a Cell Leader, you are entrusted with putting warriors into battle. Take this matter seriously. What should be taught in this training?

BASIC TRAINING PREPARES CELL MEMBERS FOR MINISTRY

Basic Training cannot be developed until a well-defined strategy has been created by your Cell Group. It must include reaching the unreached through the ministry of every member. Mastery of this task should be primary in all courses provided. Preparation times should equip believers to *make* disciples, not to just *be* disciples.

Since a Cell Church must guide believers to live a Kingdom lifestyle, knowing how to apply Scripture to daily activities is crucial. Therefore, a spiritual basic training must become a vital part of every Cell Group member's journey. Furthermore, it must be standardized so all receive the same preparation. If this is done, all soldiers will stand firm when in the battle. Creating a consistent equipping structure is mandatory to creating an effective strategy for penetrating Satan's kingdoms.

For the past several years, the pastoral team of Singapore's Faith Community Baptist Church has been developing a standardized training for new Cell Group members. One of the issues was the length of the training time. Knowing that value systems change slowly and require layer upon layer of new experiences, it was decided that the basic training should take about one year.

 Each Cell member is accountable to a Sponsor during the first modules, dealing with Christian values. Five days of self-study, involving fifteen minutes a day, is scheduled. Following a week of self-study, a weekly accountability time with the Sponsor takes place.

Each incoming Cell member is assigned to a person who has already completed the module to be completed. Thus, all learners become instructors of the same material. This pattern has significantly strengthened Cell life!

BASIC TRAINING ASSUMPTIONS

You should evaluate Cell members who enter your Cell Group and discern how they learn. What will be required to equip them for ministry? How many of these assumptions are valid for them?

1. They have never been trained to study the Bible on their own.
2. Their value systems have never been "Kingdomized."
3. They don't set a high priority on bringing unbelievers to Christ.
4. Their prayer life is either nonexistent or impotent.
5. They know little about spiritual warfare and have no experience.
6. Even when confronted by searching unbelievers, they don't know what to do.

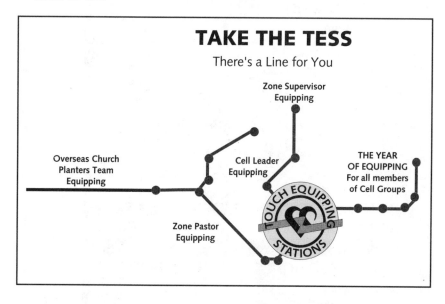

What will it take to prepare them for ministry? Rather than lectures, they will require a journey into ministry. The *Journey Guide* was created to help you evaluate the condition of the incoming Cell member and to describe each equipping module.

The TOUCH EQUIPPING STATIONS guide the Cell group members through every aspect of training. All this is explained in a *TESS CATALOG*, which must be prepared by each Cell Church to fit their own pattern. The "Year of Equipping" as developed by the Faith Community Baptist Church in Singapore is described on the next page. Most of the modules are available to other churches.

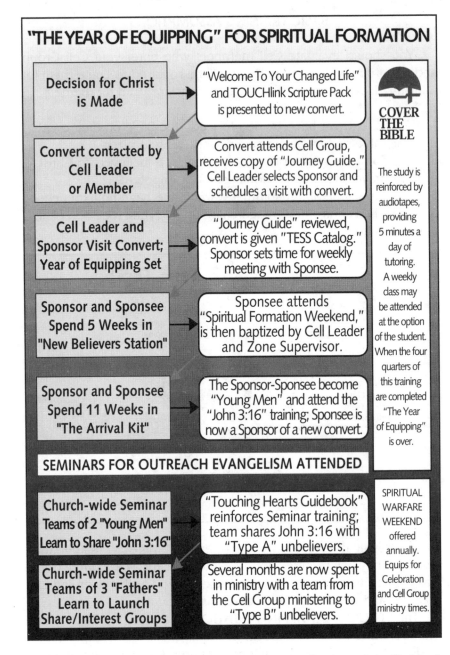

"THE YEAR OF EQUIPPING" FOR SPIRITUAL FORMATION

Decision for Christ is Made →	"Welcome To Your Changed Life" and TOUCHlink Scripture Pack is presented to new convert.	**COVER THE BIBLE**
Convert contacted by Cell Leader or Member →	Convert attends Cell Group, receives copy of "Journey Guide." Cell Leader selects Sponsor and schedules a visit with convert.	The study is reinforced by audiotapes, providing 5 minutes a day of tutoring.
Cell Leader and Sponsor Visit Convert; Year of Equipping Set →	"Journey Guide" reviewed, convert is given "TESS Catalog." Sponsor sets time for weekly meeting with Sponsee.	A weekly class may be attended at the option of the student.
Sponsor and Sponsee Spend 5 Weeks in "New Believers Station" →	Sponsee attends "Spiritual Formation Weekend," is then baptized by Cell Leader and Zone Supervisor.	When the four quarters of this training are completed "The Year of Equipping" is over.
Sponsor and Sponsee Spend 11 Weeks in "The Arrival Kit" →	The Sponsor-Sponsee become "Young Men" and attend the "John 3:16" training; Sponsee is now a Sponsor of a new convert.	

SEMINARS FOR OUTREACH EVANGELISM ATTENDED

Church-wide Seminar Teams of 2 "Young Men" Learn to Share "John 3:16" →	"Touching Hearts Guidebook" reinforces Seminar training; team shares John 3:16 with "Type A" unbelievers.	SPIRITUAL WARFARE WEEKEND offered annually.
Church-wide Seminar Teams of 3 "Fathers" Learn to Launch Share/Interest Groups →	Several months are now spent in ministry with a team from the Cell Group ministering to "Type B" unbelievers.	Equips for Celebration and Cell Group ministry times.

How should a Cell Church structure its basic training? Much depends on the way Cell members learn. In Singapore, a highly disciplined society requires the pattern similar to that shown above.

However, Mission Elim in El Salvador has 90,000 trained people, and they have virtually no printed literature in their training!

As a Cell Leader, you must not assume that putting printed material in the hands of a Cell member will equip them. Ministry is not *taught*—it's *caught!* While the equipping modules can have a powerful impact, they are worthless in imparting compassion for the lost, courage to overcome spiritual adversaries, and hearing the voice of God. This is the reason the Cell Group is central to spiritual growth and ministry.

Be careful not to make Cell members feel like they are children in a classroom while taking the "Year of Equipping." Making members feel guilty if they don't do their weekly preparation will not develop zeal for their ministry! Your attitude must be one of affirming them and demonstrating for them how to minister.

The TOUCH EQUIPPING STATIONS also provide additional training for those who complete the first year. Advanced modules provide courses in Bible, theology, counseling, etc.

The "Year of Equipping" will leave an indelible impression on the life of each new Cell member. Your visit and the assignment of a Sponsor is a clear statement that membership in the group means preparation for future ministry. Surrounded by examples of others who have completed the training, there will be a motivation to follow their journey. The result will be a mighty army!

7

The Journey Guide

Perhaps you are thinking, "I am anxious to learn about how to conduct the Cell Group meeting. When is this book going to get to the point?" If so, you are missing the point! For too long we have assumed it is a waste of time to spend time together as Christians without having an agenda. The people in your Cell are the agenda! Does the work of the Lord begin when we form a group, or organize a rally, or sponsor a mass crusade? Not at all. It begins with personal relationships. Therefore, before we talk about your directing the group's activities, we must focus on your ministry to the individuals in it.

Nothing can substitute for personal times with each member of your flock! It will be in such private times that you will discern their value systems and deepest needs. While you will usually have your Intern at your side when you visit, there will be times when even more private sessions may help you gain special insights into some persons.

To help you with the initial contacts with your flock members, a *Journey Guide* is used. It is designed to pave the way for you to talk about each person's spiritual journey. A sample of it is in the back of this book. One of these *Journey Guides* should be given to each person in the group as soon as you know he or she is joining the group. It's to be completed in private. By completing it prior to your visit, an awareness of spiritual needs will be created.

SCHEDULING THE JOURNEY GUIDE VISIT

When you present the *Journey Guide*, also select a member from the Cell who can be the Sponsor for this person. Anyone who has been a Christian just a few months longer than the newcomer will qualify. Don't be too concerned about how "mature" the Sponsor is, as long as he or she has a desire to serve the Lord. (Of course, you will always assign men to men and women to women.) When you visit, take the Sponsor along with you. Include your Intern as well.

Two things are important to remember when scheduling the visit: first, the setting; second, the time frame. The setting is all-important! Will there be complete privacy? Will little children create constant disturbances? Will the telephone interrupt you at critical moments? You never truly know a person until you meet them in their home. Usually it's best to conduct the interview there, but there can be exceptions. In these cases, meet in your home. I have even found it best in some circumstances to meet in a quiet corner of a restaurant.

The time frame should not be too limited. If the Lord opens the way for some special sharing, you will feel pressured if you have scheduled only one hour for these visits. Set the visit at a time when you will not be under stress to finish by a certain time.

CONDUCTING THE INTERVIEW

If you have not spent much time together before this, take time to get acquainted. If appropriate, share these Friendship Questions (Quaker Questions) together:
- Where did you live between the ages of seven and twelve and how many brothers and sisters did you have?
- How did you heat your house? (Or, what kind of transportation did your family usually use?)
- Who was the warmest person in your life during those years?
- When did "God" become more than just a word to you?

JOURNEY GUIDE INTERVIEW

How long a Christian? *About three years.*

Any lapses in the past? *Yes. Past several months.*

Previous Christian training? *None.*

Previous Christian service? *Served as an Usher for a few weeks.*

In past, how active in church life? *Sporadic.*

Conversion experience: questionable? *Possible confusion. Check this out!*

Faith Sharing in past? *None.*

Bible Knowledge Quiz: Score? *Has little knowledge of scripture.*

Awareness of Spiritual Gifts? *Brand new area for him, needs teaching.*

Gifts actively used? None. *Not Spirit-filled.*

Is there a consistent pattern of prayer? *None.*

Is there a consistent pattern of Bible study? *None.*

Led anyone to Christ? *No.*

How does this person learn? *Seldom reads. Must be tutored by Sponsor.*

Did material on Strongholds surface anything? *Wants to think it over.*

Any strongholds? *None disclosed, obviously present. Time is needed here.*

Aware of Cell Group lifestyle? Ready to commit? *Yes. Loves Cell.*

Feelings about having, then becoming, a Sponsor? *Scared, but willing.*

Readiness for outreach? *Will require a model to show him how.*

> After you have completed the interview and are alone, write down your thoughts about this person while they are fresh in your mind. List stress areas you have discerned. Then turn to the FORMS section and create an INTERCESSORY PRAYER LIST for this person.

THOUGHTS:

At a real crossroads. He is stressed out over the loss of his job. He has come to us with much potential, but will need much care. First step will be to help him lead an Ice Breaker. Sponsor will have to talk him through The Arrival Kit and involve him in sharing times before growth will be seen.

If these are not appropriate, use something else to "break the ice" and create openness between you.

Then, pray together, inviting the Holy Spirit to guide you as you talk about the journey you will share with one another. Ask your Intern or Sponsor to lead, then the Sponsor or the person being visited, then you close. Evaluate the way this new member prays: is it evident that prayer is a regular activity in this person's life? If not, what can you do to expose this person to those in the flock who have strong prayer habits?

Next, let the person share with you their responses to the *Journey Guide*. Examine it page by page. Follow the suggested interview outline provided in the FORMS section at the back of this book on page 241. A sample of a completed form is found on the previous page.

THE EQUIPPING MODULES

Are you a "first generation" Shepherd? If so, you have the disadvantage of not having experienced the cycle of equipping we will now discuss. At the very least, you should familiarize yourself with each module. Then, as time and opportunity permit, review or attend those which would be helpful to your own growth.

After you have completed your time of sharing, recommend appropriate Equipping Modules, described on the chart on page 71. Note that some of these modules will be provided in special seminars to be scheduled for all Cell Group members. This is true for the *Touching Hearts Guidebook* and the modules for training *Share/Interest* Group teams.

Each time a module is completed, you will be asked to sign the "Verification of Completion" form at the back of each book. At this time, pray a blessing for this person. Notify your Zone Supervisor of this progress, so it can be recorded in the Zone records.

Remember, the test of spiritual maturity is accepting responsibility. Entering and completing "The Year of Equipping" is the testing ground! Even as you conduct the initial interview with each new Cell member, be thinking about other tasks related to the life of the flock which could be given to this person. Distribute the opportunities for service equally among all, giving each person the joy of growing by serving. This can also include all but the smallest children! I recall a

Equipping Resorces Avaliable for Flock Training

Entry Level	Characteristics	Courses Offered
LITTLE CHILDREN New Believer	Recent Convert Not Grounded	New Believers Station The Arrival Kit
Ready for Service	Able to befriend a newer believer	Sponsor's Guidebook
PROBLEMED PERSONS Cold Christian	Never Discipled Lapse of many years Past disinterest about personal ministry	The Arrival Kit Sponsor's Guidebook
Lukewarm Christian	Some previous growth Value System fuzzy Not Spirit-filled	The Arrival Kit Sponsor's Guidebook
Emotionally Damaged	Strongholds Needs Deliverance Shame, Bitterness	The Arrival Kit Search for Significance

Equipping for Effective Service to Others		
FOR EVERYONE	Readiness to learn the Bible in depth	Cover The Bible
YOUNG MEN	Ready to learn to win "Type A" unbelievers	Touching Hearts Guidebook
FATHERS	Ready to learn to win "Type B" unbelievers through ministry on a Share Group Team or an Interest Group Team	Building Bridges, Building Groups, & Building Awareness, Opening Hearts Interest Groups Guidebook
WIDER MINISTRY	Ready to become a Cell Group Intern	Shepherd's Guidebook Cell Leader's Guidebook

group in which three eight year olds were responsible for serving the refreshments and drinks. This was their regular task, and they loved it! It also gave them a direct relationship to all who attended the gatherings.

REVIEW THE JOURNEY GUIDE EVALUATION FORM

Explain that the steps listed in the Evaluation Form (pages 13-14 in the *Journey Guide*) are not complete, but simply mark "milestones" on the journey. Also, they don't always come in the same order for all of us. Sooner or later, however, we will pass by each one on our journey toward spiritual maturity.

Using a yellow highlighter, color in the milestones which have already been reached. Discuss the ones which remain and recommend appropriate equipping modules to further the journey. Refer to equipping resources available for flock training, explaining the various modules and recommending a sequence to follow. Then complete page 15 in the *Journey Guide* and make a copy for your own records.

Explain that all of us remain as we are except for the people we meet and the equipping activities we undertake. Growing as a Christian is like growing as a person: there must be a proper diet, or our development is stunted. You may wish to share Hebrews 5:12-14, explaining that stunted development among Christians is not a new problem!

RECORD THE PLAN FOR GROWTH AND FOLLOW THROUGH

Commit yourself to help this person get into *The Arrival Kit.* Create the link with another group member who will serve as a Sponsor and guide for the eleven week study.

Don't relax until each flock member has been equipped for further growth and ministry! No maturing takes place when Christians are idling in neutral, when they are undeveloped and uncommitted. Shepherd, guide your sheep into green pastures.

8

The Shepherd's Prayer Life

Have you heard of J. O. Frasier? He left England many years ago to bring the message of Christ's love to the Lisus, an unreached tribal group who lived in the high mountain ranges of western China. The entry to the ranges was at their midpoint, a valley containing a small outpost village. Frasier remained there until he found a Lisu who tutored him in the dialect. After weeks of study, he discovered this Lisu was from the northern range and the dialect he was learning would best prepare him for working in that area.

Frasier realized he would probably be the only missionary to this tribe for years to come. He prayed, "Lord, which way should I go? North, or South?" His Master said, "Both. Pray for the Southern Lisus from sunup to noon and evangelize the Northern Lisus from noon to sundown."

This became the pattern of his life. For years and years, he used half of each day to intercede for Lisus in the south and used the other half to evangelize the Lisus around him. The work grew slowly. A few hundred Christians were the harvest of a decade of ministry.

After many years, he left the field for the first time to rest and get supplies in the outpost village. Now very familiar with the tribal tongue, he heard a Lisu speaking with a different dialect in the marketplace. He had met his first Southern Lisu! Lovingly, Frasier invited the man to come and stay with him in his rented quarters. As he heard the message of Jesus, the Lisu was quick to respond and accept Him as his Lord and Savior.

For several weeks, Frasier tutored the illiterate man, helping him to memorize passages of scripture. He told him story after story from the Bible, always praying that the Spirit would sharpen his ability to remember what he was hearing.

As the men parted, Frasier urged him to tell all the Southern Lisus about Jesus. He then returned to the site of his own ministry, praying as usual for half of each day for those to the south. Years passed . . . and then a delegation of Southern Lisus arrived at his village. They reported the news that thousands of Southern Lisus had followed Christ and were in desperate need of someone to come and teach them more!

As tears of joy welled up in his eyes, the missionary realized his time invested in prayer from sunup to noon had caused a harvest hundreds of times greater than all his labors from noon to sundown. It was as though God was saying, "Not by might, nor by power, but by My Spirit, shall the Lisus be reached."

Shepherd, you may experience that same result through your own prayer life! Spend consistent time with your Lord, using prayer to the utmost in your ministry. Model this by including your Intern in these times whenever possible, even as Jesus did when He took the disciples to the mountains and prayed all night.

There are a number of excellent books on prayer you may wish to read. One of the best is *Touch the World through Prayer*, by Wesley L. Duewel (Zondervan Publishers). Another one is Jack Hayford's *Prayer is Invading the Impossible* (Logos).

If you want to learn to pray with power and effect, pray! Nothing will bring you a greater thirst for prayer than actually doing it. Set regular periods for prayer into your schedule. If you have to make a choice between praying and doing, choose to pray. You will achieve more in your ministry, because you took the time to pray.

There are so many facets to praying that this single chapter is like a drop of water falling into the ocean. However, from your perspective it is important to consider three areas as beginning points:

PRAYER: THE LISTENING ROOM

In this diagram, the wrong way to pray is illustrated. The Shepherd is deciding "what's best" in a given situation. Going to prayer (A), God is then asked to use His power and resources to cause "what's best" to happen. When things don't develop as desired, the Shepherd then goes to the "Holy Man (B)— usually a pastor or someone who is considered to have a stronger relationship with God—and he is asked to secure God's cooperation.

A Christian's prayer can be built on this pattern that makes man the decision maker—the "Master"—and turns God into a servant, who must respond by obeying the desires of the one praying.

Obviously, this type of praying will see few results. God does not begin His relationship with us by sublimating His will to our wills. Has your own prayer life followed this pattern in the past? If so, it may explain why so few prayers have been answered.

There is an important change to be made. We never decide "what's best." That's not what servants do; masters make decisions. Then, servants execute these decisions. Thus, we must draw a new diagram.

In this diagram, the Shepherd is first seeking to know the will of God concerning a situation. Prayer becomes a "Listening Room" experience. It is not possible to do the will of God without praying according to His will. Then, with absolute assurance, the "binding on earth of what is bound in heaven" takes place. Praying takes on an entirely new perspective when we learn how to approach the Throne of God in this manner.

Jesus is our example for the importance of hearing God before we take action. He said,

> For I did not speak of my own accord, but the Father who sent me commanded me what to say and how to say it.
> ·John 12:49

Even our Lord needed a Listening Room! That's why He prayed through the night hours and fasted for forty days. He encouraged his disciples to pray with him. In another passage, he defined those who are His true family when He said,

> "My mother and brothers are those who hear God's word and put it into practice." ·Luke 8:21

James reminds us,

> If any of you lacks wisdom, he should ask God, who gives generously to all without finding fault and it will be given to him. ·James 1:5

Developing good habits for listening, the first phase of prayer, is an important advance in the Christian walk. In *Hearing God*, Peter Lord writes:

> A key to hearing God's promises and acting as though they were already so is to command your mind, based on something God has said . . . There are three steps to this process:
>
> 1. Make a deliberate choice and effort to set your mind on God. Ask his help if you think you have an undisciplined mind.
> 2. Make a deliberate choice to exercise your mind in focusing on God. The best way is to have a regular time to pursue this intensely. Like any other form of exercise, begin at a low level and increase gradually.
> 3. Carry this exercise of setting your mind on God into every area of life. Do it by determining to consciously bring every thought captive to God and immediately turning to God in all circumstances.

Imagine you are a carpenter, hired by a wealthy man to build a house. He shows you the blueprints, points to the foundation and tells you to proceed. "Wait a minute!" you say: "You have forgotten something. Where are the boards and the nails?" He says to you, "Oh . . . use your own boards and nails. I have other concerns now; you take it from here. Use your own resources."

Silly, isn't it? Yet, much of the activity we do for our Lord is done with what we consider to be our own resources. (Of course, a true servant knows that everything inside his skin and every possession outside his skin is the property of his Master.) Too often, we consider solutions which provide the best man can offer, rather than the power of God.

In Abidjan, Ivory Coast, Jack Taylor and I were asked to pray for a precious little three year old girl who had been deaf from birth. We did so, without the time required to go to the Listening Room about the matter. Our prayers were not answered. Later that evening, I said to Ruthie, "Perhaps the most Christian thing we can do for that child is to pay to bring her to Houston for a complete examination by specialists." I was thinking my thoughts, not God's thoughts. I was considering my resources, not God's resources.

The next day, Easter Sunday, 1988, a team of workers from the Cell Church entered into fervent prayer which brought deliverance from deafness to this girl. When we next saw her she was crying in fright at the loud sounds made by a nearby band, hands clapped over her ears! Entering a world of noises was a brand new experience for her. For me, it was a brand new lesson in the power of prayer.

When Jesus sent the seventy into Perea, He told them not to take any extra shoes, coats, or coins. All the resources they needed would have to come from the Master. Power to heal, to cast out demons, to set prisoners free, would come from above. We, too, must learn to do the work of God using the resources of God.

There will be many times in your ministry as a Shepherd when there will be a need for a physical healing, for an impossible marital conflict to be ended, or for a rebellious person's life to be changed. Leave the practice of psychology and medicine to those trained in those skills, making referrals as needed.

For your ministry, learn to receive and dispense the resources of your Lord and Master. If you ask Him for bread, He has promised He will not give you a stone. We receive not because we ask not, or because we ask amiss. He is more willing to give than we are to receive. Learn how to listen, and then learn how to receive. You will never be quite the same person again after you hear, in your prayer time, the inner voice of the Spirit saying, "I have heard you. Your prayer is answered. The resource is given. Stop praying and begin to praise. The mission is accomplished!"

PRAYER: THE TOOL OF WARFARE

In *The Kingdom Factor*, Roger Mitchell writes:

> Spiritual warfare is the hidden face of evangelism. This is actually obvious from the life of Jesus, in particular from the context of the temptations, his explanation of the need to bind the strong man in order to see the kingdom come powerfully and his comments to the disciples about why he was successful in casting out a demon when they were not.

When I left seminary, I had lost my belief in the existence of a personal devil or the existence of demons in today's world. I was a sitting duck on a pond for Beelzebub's manipulations! That is no longer true. My first confrontation with the demonic was in the company of a God-fearing psychiatrist who brought a possessed woman to my office. When the woman saw a painting of Christ on the wall, she began to scream as though we were peeling off her skin with a blunt knife.

My second confrontation came in Belo Horizonte, Brazil, where a man writhed in agony in the middle of a service in the First Baptist Church as I preached on the blood of Christ. Later that evening, a missionary and I saw that man totally set free from his possession, the result of his mother dedicating him to Satan as a baby. The joy that flooded his soul as Christ replaced the powers that had oppressed him for years was a precious sight.

Since then, I have witnessed and interviewed many who have been delivered from strongholds. Unquestionably, every life is a battleground between the power of the devil and the power of Christ. For too long, the church has refused to enter into the fray. Shepherd, it will not be long until you will come into situations where it should be obvious your warfare is not against flesh and blood, but against principalities and powers of the air. Consider this scripture:

When they came to the crowd, a man approached Jesus and knelt before him. "Lord, have mercy on my son," he said. "He has seizures and is suffering greatly. He often falls into the fire or into the water. I brought him to your disciples, but they could not heal him." "O unbelieving and perverse generation," Jesus replied, "how long shall I stay with you? How long shall I put up with you? Bring the boy here to me." Jesus rebuked the demon and it came out of the boy and he was healed from that moment. Then the disciples came to Jesus in private and asked, "Why couldn't we drive it out?" He replied, "Because you have so little faith. I tell you the truth, if you have faith as small as a mustard seed, you can say to this mountain, 'Move from here to there' and it will move. Nothing will be impossible for you. But this kind does not go out except by prayer and fasting." •Matthew 17:14-21 (KJV)

"Prayer and fasting . . . " here's a reference to prayer so intense that normal bodily nourishment is set aside because of an urgent matter! When soldiers are in battle, they do not pay attention to the normal processes of life. Such is the case in spiritual warfare.

You will need to discover and maintain a balance between prayer as warfare and prayer as intercession. Among the gifts of the Spirit is the ability to distinguish between true and false spirits. The matter of dealing with strongholds is a ministry you will undoubtedly do with others. As with all other ministry skills, it's necessary for you to become an apprentice to someone who has walked ahead of you in these matters.

Here is an example: Her daughter was in total rebellion. The teenager had slipped out the back door with a suitcase and had been gone for ten days. The mother was frantic. Calls to all her friends had been fruitless. If they knew her whereabouts, they were not talking. Was she dead, raped, drugged, unconscious? Sleep was impossible. Food went untouched. Finally, the woman called her Cell Group to come over and pray with her. All felt her burden and together they began to pray with urgency. The session ended with each member taking a specific time period to continue praying, around the clock, for the girl. Eighteen hours later, the runaway knocked on the front door of her home. "Mother, I have never been so miserable in my life. I have felt as though God Himself was whispering in my ear, telling me to come home. I want to talk to you. I want to be different."

That Cell Group had experienced the power of prayer as a tool of warfare. Do you have any doubts about their further involvement in the life of that daughter? She was nourished and loved by them all and set free from the power of cocaine, heavy metal music and shallow morals.

In Ezekiel 47, the prophet is shown a vision of water flowing from the temple. He waded out into it: first, ankle deep, then knee deep, then up to his waist and then so deep he had to swim in it. In the same way, your journey will take you into the glorious power of Christ a little at a time. You will discover His riches are greater than you ever dreamed and His power to break strongholds more than you will ever require. Be filled with expectations, for He has brought you to this time of servant ministry to overflow your life with His own. Dr. Peter Wagner has written several books about spiritual mapping. You will profit from reading them and leading your Cell Group to conduct prayer walks in the areas where you live.

PRAYER: "IT'S AMAZING WHAT PRAISING CAN DO!"

Letting circumstances take control of your life is a sure way to get ulcers. A sure cure for them is praise! Psalm 100:4 instructs us to "enter His courts with praise." It should begin every prayer session. It is not an unnecessary preface to more important things to come—it's the most important part of all.

Wesley Duewel writes in *Touching the World Through Prayer*:

Have you ever realized that God's answers to your prayers are at times delayed because you do not praise Him enough? Have you realized that mountains of difficulty often remain before you because you have failed to praise Him? Did you know you can often rout Satan faster by praise than in any other way unless it be by the command of faith? Or that the command of faith is often related to a praise barrage? Did you know that depression can be lifted by the sacrifice of persistent praise? Praise pierces the darkness, dynamites long standing obstructions and send the demons of hell fleeing.

INTERCESSORY PRAYER LIST

Cell Group Member: **Philip Tan**

Stress Areas: **Lost his job 6 months ago. Father died 3 months ago.**

Date	Prayer Need	By Faith, I See This Person:
7 / 7 / 94 ASKED 9 / 2 / 94 ANSWERED	Strongholds: unable to handle strong feelings of anger toward his former employer.	Able to recognize his significance is not based on his achievements but upon his status as a child of God.
Date	Prayer Need	By Faith, I See This Person:
10 / 2 / 94 ASKED 12 / 21/ 94 ANSWERED	Wants to share his faith with his father, but afraid of the rejection he will face.	Bold and tactful in his faith-sharing, gaining the respect of his father, winning him to Jesus!
Date	Prayer Need	By Faith, I See This Person:
__ / __ / __ ASKED __ / __ / __ ANSWERED		
Date	Prayer Need	By Faith, I See This Person:
__ / __ / __ ASKED __ / __ / __ ANSWERED		
Date	Prayer Need	By Faith, I See This Person:
__ / __ / __ ASKED __ / __ / __ ANSWERED		
Date	Prayer Need	By Faith, I See This Person:
__ / __ / __ ASKED __ / __ / __ ANSWERED		

Jack Taylor, author of *The Hallelujah Factor,* teaches we should praise God for three things: for who He is, for what He has done and for what He is about to do. By focusing on His glory and His mighty deeds, the puny circumstances which seem so depressing are neutralized. It's a glorious thing to sing prayer praises, to speak prayer praises, to experience praise in all ways possible. As you grow into this lifestyle as a person, your Cell Group will also begin to know the power and joy of praise.

You will regularly begin your Cell Group meetings with a time of praise, singing, praying, reading psalms aloud together. When you go to the group meetings, don't just go prayed up; go praised up!

PRAYER: BY FAITH, BELIEVING IT'S SO WHEN IT'S NOT SO

In the FORMS section of this book, you'll find a sheet like the one on page 81, which has been filled out to illustrate its usefulness. Note that it lists the stress points in the life of this person. The next chapter will explain that in detail. The Shepherd dated each request as he began his intercession and dated it again when the prayer as it was answered. At the same time he wrote out the prayer request, he also went to the Listening Room and asked his Lord for an awareness of how the prayer would be answered. He then recorded this in the area of the form marked "BY FAITH, I SEE THIS PERSON:"

HERE'S A TRUE REPORT OF WHAT
PRAYER DID IN A CELL GROUP

When he first came to our group, he had a serious drinking problem. He shared that he had followed the Lord as a boy, but had spent many years apart from Him. As the weeks passed, he became hungry for the things of God and finally stepped into a beautiful new relationship with Christ.

It was then he asked me to have lunch with him. After we ordered he said, "I'm living with a woman. Now that I have come to new life in Christ, I know I need to break it off, but I am afraid of her. Once before, I left her. She got drunk and came to the auto parts store where I worked. She picked up a tire jack and started swinging it, breaking out store windows and knocking down racks of merchandise. I tried to stop her, and she ripped off my shirt, digging her fingernails into my chest until I needed over a hundred stitches. It took seven policemen to get her handcuffed and into the paddy wagon. She has told me she will kill me if I try to leave her. I don't know what to do."

I said, "Let's ask the Lord to show her what He is going to do in her life. First of all, let's list the strongholds Satan has in her life." I turned my paper place mat over and began to write as we talked: "Strongholds: drunkenness, rage, jealousy, fear. Terrible self-image. Unforgiving toward husband who abandoned her, fearful of being abandoned again. Spirit of murder."

We then went to the Listening Room, asking the Spirit to let us see her as she would become after Christ had delivered her. I wrote, "In love with her Lord, chaste and sober, devoted to her two daughters, active in Christian service."

My friend looked stunned! "I really can't believe the woman I sleep with will ever be like that, but I am willing to trust the Lord by faith to make it happen." We began the first of many prayer times for her, attacking satanic strongholds and rejoicing in what would be so for her, which was not yet so! As we got into our cars, I said, "Invite her to the Cell Group tonight. We're meeting in my house. Just tell her she has to come with you. She'll do it." He looked at me like I had lost my mind. "Okay, I'll ask her . . . but she's not going to agree." I said, "Quit looking at the circumstances and begin to see through the eyes of faith!"

She came with him, frightened as a kitten in a thunderstorm. The women in the group hugged her as they served her coffee and cake. We devoted the entire evening to getting acquainted with her and she with us. Using the Quaker Questions, we learned about her girl-hood, her marriage to the father of her two daughters and how he abandoned them. We fought back our own tears as she shared how they had migrated illegally to Houston from Mexico and what a rough battle she had faced as she gained employment and made a home for them.

The next week, she returned to our group and brought her delightful teen-aged daughter with her. The girl was an excellent athlete and brought along several trophies she had won. We proudly displayed them in the breakfast bar of the house we were meeting in and ended with prayer for her future and her desire to go to college.

In about six weeks, my friend returned to the apartment he shared with the woman and her daughters after work. His clothes had been carefully laundered, ironed and packed in his suitcases. The woman said, "I have now become a Christian and will be baptized in the Iglesia Bautista this Sunday. I cannot live with you any more. You must leave us. I truly love you, but if we are to continue to see each other it must only be with purity of relationships whenever we are together."

Prayer had torn down strongholds and had set her free! You will soon have many stories like this one as a result of your own Cell Group activity. Step into deeper waters, friend. Wade out until you are swimming in the current of God's activity. There are some exciting things ahead for you!

MAKE A LIST OF PRAYER NEEDS

Pray for God to:
- Deepen hunger for God in members of the group.
- Reveal Himself more fully to the flock. (This is always needed for spiritual growth.)
- Produce a discontent with lifestyles which are contrary to Him.
- Quicken faith to believe He is going to do the unseen.
- Give the flock new sensitivity to unreached persons.
- Prepare key individuals He is planning to use.
- Pray for your own needs and those of your family members.
- Enlarge your vision of the Body of Christ and your love for it.
- Enlarge His church worldwide by changing dead structures.

In Peter Lord's life, prayer became operative in a special way. His experience with prayer has impacted thousands of lives. In his handbook on prayer, *The 2959 Plan*, he says:

> It is honoring to God when our immediate and first response to any situation is to consult Him. It is very dishonoring to God when we make Him our last choice. Have you ever heard someone say, "We have done all we can, we might as well pray." If we are going to "acknowledge Him in all our ways" and ". . . seek first the Kingdom of God," one of the best ways is to make Him our Consultant and Advisor.

Prayer Chain

Name _Write your name here_

Phones: (H) **497 7901** (W) **496 0202**

Name _Intern's name goes here_

Phones: (H) **465 3408** (W) **777 5864**

Name _Floyd Johnson_

P

Photocopy this form from sample found in the
FORMS section of this book. Fill it out with names of
all Cell members and give a copy to each person.
Your name is always the first one on the Prayer
Chain, followed by your Intern's name. Anyone can
start the chain by calling the person below their
name. If someone cannot be reached, the next
name on the list is called. The last person on the list
calls you back to notify you all links have been
made.

Phones: (H) **364 8749** (W) **874 5621**

Name _Christina Chua_

Phones: (H) **436 8912** (W) **823 5599**

Name _Joey Beckham_

Phones: (H) **965 3419** (W) **254 7698**

CREATING THE FLOCK'S PRAYER CHAIN

You will find Prayer Chain forms in the back of this book, ready to use with your flock. As the example on page 85 indicates, it creates a way for people to rapidly contact one another to share prayer needs. A copy of it should be given to each member. If a person next on the list is "out of pocket," the name following should then be called.

The chain should be prayerfully developed by the group, not just announced as an add-on to a meeting. Spend time talking about ways the chain will be used:

• Day or night, it's available when a crisis hits a member of the flock.
• It can call the group to intercession when an unbeliever being culti-vated is at a point of commitment and a member will be "drawing in the net."
• It binds the group together in special experiences of its members, such as a member taking tests for cancer.

Prayer Chains are vital to spiritually bind members together. In the weeks which follow, it will be used in the middle of the day and in the middle of the night. On some occasions, the message sent through it may actually call the group together for an emergency time of group intercession.

For example, a group's life was shattered when one of the wives was driving home from the store with her little girl in the seat beside her. A truck went through an intersection and slammed into them. The Shepherd was called and before leaving for the hospital trig-gered the Prayer Chain. Upon reaching the hospital, he discovered the life of the wife was hanging by a thread. He realized his pres-ence at the hospital was not as vital as prayer at that point. Leaving his Intern with the husband, he called the flock to meet at his house. Through the evening, they stayed before the Lord in intercession for their beloved lady. About midnight, the Intern called to inform the group that the crisis had been passed, internal bleeding had stopped and the doctor felt she would pull through.

One caution: some groups may include a person who has poor judgment about what should be put on the prayer chain. Therefore, either you or your Intern should be the ones to set it in motion. All calls come to you first!

9

"Kinning:" Creating Christian Kinfolk

Kinning: it's a good word! People who enter your Cell Group need to feel you have become like "kinfolks" to them. Everyone feeling they are part of the family of Christ is important.

Someone has said, "Home is where you can always come to, whether you have been good or bad and know you won't be kicked out." One of your tasks will be to make each new member feel secure in their new Cell Group relationships. If a newcomer is not made to feel welcome and at home within three visits, they will typically drop out.

It takes two things to accomplish "kinning:" love and special investments of time. You see, you will never shepherd a person until you have taken time to know them!

After you have received the name of a person who is interested in attending your Cell Group, or as soon as a guest is brought by an existing member, you may wish to do any combination of the following:

1. Visit in the person's home. Meet all the people who live there.
2. Telephone the person and make a date to have lunch together.
3. Sit together in Congregation or Celebration gatherings.
4. Share in some fun times: picnic, tennis, shopping, sports, etc.

Here are some things which will develop relationships between the members of the Cell Group:

1. Ask three people in the group to drop by and visit or telephone twice in one week visitors and new members.
2. Encourage existing group members to personally invite the new visitor to attend the next meeting.
3. Sometimes a new member feels like they have to "crash" our group because we tend to arrive and migrate to those we already know. Members must give highest priority to making newcomers feel comfortable in their midst.

One of the things about a true family is its willingness to let each person be who they are. Your Cell Group can be such a family.

CELL GROUPS AND "OIKOS CONNECTIONS"

Oikos: one's "primary group." The word is found repeatedly in the New Testament and is usually translated "household." However, it doesn't just refer to family members. Every one of us have a "primary group" of friends who relate directly to us through family, work, recreation, hobbies and neighbors. These are the persons we talk to, relate to, share with for at least a total of one hour each week.

We may know as many as two hundred people by name and may have occasional relationships with several dozen. However, it is unusual to find a person who has as many as twenty people in their *oikos*, their primary group. A recent survey of Christians revealed they averaged about nine such people and a large percentage of them had not developed a new *oikos* relationship in six months.

Life is made up of endless chains of *oikos* connections. Every person in your Cell Group is already entwined in these relationships. Newcomers feel very much "outside" when they visit your group for the first time, unless they have established an *oikos* connection with one of them. If they are not "kinned" by the members, they will not stay very long or try very hard to be included before they return to their old friends.

OIKOS SIZES VARY WIDELY,
BASED ON EMOTIONAL STRENGTH

The size of an *oikos* depends on the capacity of a person to carry on relationships with others. Those who have been deeply scarred emotionally may have only three to five people in their *oikos*, while those with unstressed past lives will have larger ones. Sadly, those who most need love and friendship are those with the least opportunity to receive it. Each person lives within a primary *oikos* group and is strongly influenced by it. Thus, it is important for you to take time to meet as many of the *oikos* people as possible and to at least have an impression about the rest of them. This can be initiated during the *Journey Guide* interview and will be developed as you focus on oikoses in a Cell Group session.

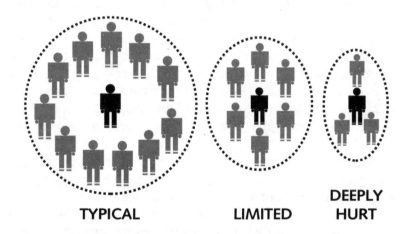

TYPICAL   **LIMITED**   **DEEPLY HURT**

Sad, but true . . . many an unchurched person got as far as the first contact with Christians, only to feel "outside," unloved. Don't let that happen in your group.

Are you aware that about fifty per cent of all church members are inactive? How does this happen? Imagine the shift in these people: they come into church membership happy, excited, filled with hope for a new walk with Christ. They seek to make new friends, at the same time explaining to their *oikos* group why they have shifted their lifestyles. Imagine the stress which accompanies this situation!

Perhaps the situation develops like this: many Christians shake hands with them. A few call them by name when they see them. A Sunday School worker urges them to become regular in a class.

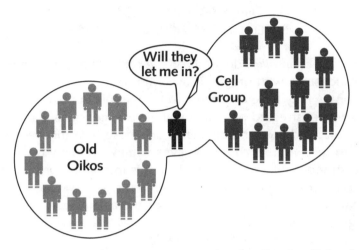

Again, warm welcomes are given by the Sunday School class members, but no one offers to go out to lunch with the new member and no one ever telephones—with the one exception of the "Inreach Director" of the class, who constantly calls to be sure the person is planning to attend the class next Sunday: "It's High Attendance Day. We really need you!" For what? For the attendance record? Then, it's time for the annual Stewardship Drive. Finally, a visit takes place from the Deacon's Committee, to pick up the pledge card!

Who are these dropouts? Many of them are the shy people who don't readily make friends. All of them were searching for a deeper walk with the Lord. None of them realized at the start that such a deeper walk is embedded in community and in deep relationships and none of them found what they were looking for in the church. Now confused, they drop out. Perhaps they are bitter because their attempt to meet God in a greater way failed. Few are able to think through the dynamics of what has taken place. They simply conclude that they are not acceptable to God and that they have such drab personalities that other people do not want to be close to them.

Meanwhile, the organizational church cranks on, with about ten to twelve per cent of all the members doing ninety per cent of all the volunteer work and contributing ninety per cent of the money needed to keep the programs moving.

If your Cell Group duplicates this impersonal lifestyle, it would be better for it to be cast into the sea with a great millstone tied around its neck! Yet, it can happen so subtly that the damage is done before it is realized. Consider this description of a true church:

> *All the believers were one in heart and mind. No one claimed that any of his possessions was his own, but they shared everything they had. With great power the apostles continued to testify to the resurrection of the Lord Jesus and much grace was upon them all. There were no needy persons among them. For from time to time those who owned lands or houses sold them, brought the money from the sales and put it at the apostles' feet and it was distributed to anyone as he had need. Joseph, a Levite from Cyprus, whom the apostles called Barnabas (which means Son of Encouragement), sold a field he owned and brought the money and put it at the apostles' feet.* •Acts 4:32-37

While a Cell Group has a formal weekly gathering, its life is really embedded in the daily relationships and mutual sharing of lives. For that reason, its size simply must not exceed fifteen persons—but that's not the critical factor. More important is participation. There must be an adequate involvement of all the members in the life of the group. When the community grows larger than fifteen, this becomes difficult.

THIS IS A TRUE STORY OF HOW
ONE CELL GROUP MINISTERED:

She was a young mother, pregnant with her second child. She was also a "husband batterer." When she would fly into fits of rage, her husband would try to defend himself from her fists and scratching nails, frying pans, or whatever was nearby which could be thrown. He had lived with this for four years, meekly trying to appease her and keep her anger from erupting.

Then, at the bank where he worked, a lonely divorcee encouraged him to take her out to lunch. Her warmth, loneliness and gentle behavior captivated him. Before he knew what had happened, he was embroiled in an affair. When his wife found out, she went berserk! Thus, a few days before the birth of their second child, he moved into an apartment.

When the affair was discovered at the bank, both he and the girl were fired. The situation became more and more miserable. He spent time with his wife at the hospital, helped her bring the baby home and returned to his empty apartment.

Six months before, they had linked themselves to a Cell Group. The other young couples in the group had struggled with what to do about this situation for many weeks. They had privately counseled both the wife and the husband, and they had fervently prayed for Christ to restore the home. Finally, on a Friday night, all the children in the group were farmed out to relatives and friends for the week end. As the wives arrived at the house of the young mother, their husbands knocked on the door of the apartment where the husband was living. They drove him to his house, pulled sleeping bags out of their car trunks and announced: "We are here for an indefinite period of time. Our Lord does not want your lives to be destroyed like this. We are going to talk, to pray, to do whatever we have to do—and we are not going to leave until you two get your lives straightened out and establish a decent home for these babies!"

By Sunday morning, the exhausted group had broken through. For the first time in her life, the wife had faced the strongholds in her life and had been set free from their power. With guidance from their group, they had remembered their first love for one another and why they had married. Christ was enthroned in their lives, and they were ready to grow in grace!

A CELL GROUP IS A LIFESTYLE, NOT JUST A WEEKLY MEETING

Your Cell Group is a small Christian community. Jesus Christ has formed each of these living Cells and He is truly its Head. Perhaps you have experienced, or have observed, small groups in the church that sprang up quickly and disappeared just as rapidly. The reason? There was no true community: no renewal of persons, no ministry, no sacrificial love for others. These groups were simply meetings, gathering on Sunday or Wednesday nights. Sometimes they piously reveled in their spirituality while ignoring the need-filled people around them. No room was made for the Cross.

"Kinning" is creating true Christian community. It is home, where you are always welcome no matter what stupid decision you have made in the past or the present. It's a place where crotchety, disagreeable, thankless old sinners are welcomed and challenged to be free from their inner strongholds. Praise and worship shape its personality. The Lord's Supper, prayer, the Word of God, are all vital to its lifestyle. It is missionary, reaching out to others until it must multiply and become two Cells.

As people gather to form the Cell Group, there is no fixed pattern for how they will adjust to community life. You must start from where they are. Some will have previous experiences of living and working with other Christians in true community, while others will find the entire experience a brand new lifestyle. Those who have never been a part of a warm family unit, who have lived lives of self-sufficiency for many years and who have been betrayed in trust relationships, will need special encouragement. "Kinning" takes many forms, as many as there are individual personalities. These people cannot be developed by you. They must develop them-selves. All you can do is provide the environment for this to take place. That's why it's important for you to quickly provide specific tasks and ministries for all who are entering the Cell Group. Remember—becoming mature means becoming responsible. A person who is being useful is feeling worthwhile. Those who are simply expected to "be present" will soon fade away.

Like a marriage, after the honeymoon your group will have to work hard at the relationship if it is to be successful. The gold, silver and precious stones in your Cell Group will not be found sitting on the surface. To discover them, there must be the digging out of deep spiritual relationships.

Do you know what your best quality will be as a Shepherd? Consistency. Loving all, not some, of the group; caring as much about the life of the community this week as you did last week; transparently confessing your own shortfalls while revealing your growing faith—these are the characteristics of consistency.

Accepting persons where they are, challenging them to grow, trying to create community favorable to growth, knowing when to let go and let people grow apart from you, incorporating all into one family—that's kinning! In the weeks ahead, you will learn more about it from experience than from reading this chapter. The journey continues . . .

10

Reaching the
Unreached

Put pointedly, the purpose and goal of our Lord is to draw all men to Himself. If we are servants in any sense of the word, if we are obedient in any definition of the word, we must be totally involved in what He desires.

I have travelled over this globe studying Cell Churches. In Australia, one Baptist leader wrote about small groups in church life by suggesting that "one wheel's off and the axle's broken." In England, one large movement totally abandoned their small groups, after seeing growth to several thousand members because of them. In Little Rock, Arkansas, small groups were so successful that over sixty per cent of the church had enthusiastically endorsed them. Then the pastor phased them out because they had become stagnant. In another major church, the small groups were deliberately organized to keep people together for two years before they would multiply. In that case, the groups were supposed to be "holding tanks" for those attracted by services with special attractions. In every single one of these cases, the groups created were nothing but "navel gazing units," having no intention of winning the lost. They were all doomed from the beginning.

I have also seen churches like *L'eglise Protestante Baptiste Oeuvres et Mission* in Abidjan, Ivory Coast, Africa. It began in 1976, floundered until 1979 and then began to experiment with Cells. By 1983, they had grown to 350 and had trained the task force necessary to blanket Abidjan from their humble site in a slum area. Unlike the groups described above, this church had a passion for souls. As this is being written in April, 1994, this single church has grown to approach 45,000 in Cell membership. Some Cells multiply in only two to three month's time as a result of conversion growth. A convert is given six months of personal care before being baptized and eighteen months later will typically become a Cell Leader of a group.

Shepherd, your flock must reach out. It can be like a Cell in that African church! In six to nine months in most cultures, your Cell Group should have an attendance bumping fifteen on a consistent basis. It will then be time to multiply into two Cells. In order to reach this goal, your own heart must have a deep yearning for the lost to be brought to Christ. Does it?

DEAD ENDS: GUILT TRIPS AND "STRANGER EVANGELISM"

You have probably had your share of "guilt trips" from sermons which laid you low because you were not winning the lost. What good did they do? Have we ever done anything well because we were motivated by guilt?

Or, you may have been the victim of a witness training course. Several are making the rounds these days (they change titles about every ten years). Did you learn how to meet a total stranger, ask three questions and unload a memorized speech on the unbeliever? Did you try it? How often before you lost momentum and moved on to something else in church life?

There is no question that some are being reached through "stranger evangelism." Perhaps you yourself were brought to Jesus using that pattern. When should it be used?

We are reminded that Jesus used this pattern when he won the Samaritan woman. We are told, "He went to a well, shared the Gospel with her, she was converted and went to get all her friends to meet Jesus." Not quite! First of all, He supernaturally knew she needed help: he had a moral necessity, says the Greek, to go to Samaria. Secondly, after some small talk, He super-naturally put His finger on the sorest spot in her life: she had been through five husbands and was now simply living with a man. He entered her heart through her desperate need!

Sin is like the sting of a bee: it hurts, it occupies our thoughts and needs immediate attention. Since every person has "bee stings," God turns Satan's deception into the place for the entry of saving grace. Therefore, our first task in winning people to Christ is to head for the hurt. The last task is to explain how one may be saved.

We must earn the right to be entrusted with the facts about the "bee stings." If there is no knowledge of Christ's love or His mighty power to deliver us from strongholds, we must plant seeds of truth in the person who perishes. This may require time, prevailing prayer and many close contacts.

When one runs across an unbeliever who is hurting, searching, longing for inner peace, he or she is at the final stage before conversion. It is most appropriate to share the Gospel of peace immediately. I have done so on many airplane trips. But only Heaven knows how many unbelievers have been vaccinated against Christian friendships by our habit of pouncing on people, unloading our memorized words and walking away! Those who quote the glowing statistics of conversions from their hit-and-run methods should be required by law to also report those who were left behind, wounded. The ministry of evangelism is the ministry of the good Samaritan Jesus referred to, who stopped to nurture a battered victim of robbers. Satan is the thief, and he seldom steals a life without leaving it wounded. Our task is to bring good news to the poor, bind up the broken, bring sight to the blind and release captives. In this ministry of caring, strangers become friends and are lovingly introduced to Jesus Christ as Savior and Lord.

Consider the similarity between a Billy Graham crusade and a personal evangelism encounter. Both approaches seem to have striking similarities. In both cases, strangers hear a presentation from an evangelist. The invitation is given. Some respond, some do not, and the meeting ends. Why did some respond while others did not? Obviously, all were equally drawn by the Spirit of God. He does not go about selecting some for salvation, rejecting others:

The Lord is not slow in keeping his promise, as some understand slowness. He is patient with you, not wanting anyone to perish, but everyone to come to repentance.
•2 Peter 3:9

Those who were "Type A" unbelievers were harvested. Those who were "Type B" were not. Less than three per cent of unbelievers attend a Billy Graham crusade by themselves. Virtually all of those who make decisions have been cultivated for weeks or months by someone who loved and prayed for them.

If you look at the evidence, it becomes obvious that whenever, wherever, a person has a hunger for God, they may be readily brought to personal faith. In Acts, this was true for the Ethiopian eunuch and also for Cornelius. But for others, there must be seed planted and watered before there is a harvest. The assignment of your Cell Group is to focus on the planting and watering, knowing that the harvesting is simply plucking ripe fruit.

WORDS, WORKS and WONDERS

Roger Mitchell of London's Ichthus Fellowship writes in *The Kingdom Factor*:

It was not only the words that Jesus said that revealed the Father's glory, but the works that he did. This was so thoroughly true that Jesus could say in John 14:10, 'The words that I say to you I do not speak on my own authority; but the Father who dwells in me does his works.' We might have expected Jesus to have said either 'the works that I do I don't do on my own authority . . . ' or else 'but the Father who dwells in me speaks his words'. But he mixes the two, the words and the works. It was all together the word. So it must be with us. The good news, is what Jesus said and did. Our good news, our evangelism, consists of what we say and do.

When we share the words without the works of love, the deed is often meaningless and is often hypocritical. Vance Havner used to tell about the cat who was walking down the street in sub zero weather. It saw an open door, entered a house and saw a fireplace aglow with burning logs. It curled up in front of it and froze to death. You see, the fire was artificially produced with light bulbs and red cellophane! Words without works are like that. It makes our job much tougher, for a high percentage of unreached people today have been exposed to the false fires of the church in the past, and they are running scared.

Notice in Mark's Gospel the careful intertwining of words and works in the ministry of Jesus. He teaches, He works; He teaches, He works. Never does the one occur without the other preceding or following. So it must be with your personal life and the life of your Cell Group.

Women Cell Group members of Seoul's Full Gospel Central Church combine their marketing with sharing. As they stand before a food stall, they listen to the conversations between shopkeepers and customers. "Mrs. Lee," says the woman tending the stall, "How is your husband?" The customer's eyes cloud with tears: "He is not well. This is the second week he has had to stay home from work. I am so worried!" The Christian lady approaches her: "Mrs. Lee, I am Mrs. Tan. I am so sorry to hear about your husband. I share your pain!" Then Mrs. Tan walks home with Mrs. Lee, listening and sympathetically nodding her head. She now knows where Mrs. Lee lives! She has fervent prayer with her for her husband there on the street and departs to tell her Cell Group about this new prayer need she has discovered. The entire group begins to intercede for Mr. Lee. Mrs. Tan returns to the Lee home with another Cell member and again prayer is offered. Mrs. Lee is invited to the Cell meeting and comes. She is astonished to learn there that this group of strangers have been fervently praying for her husband. She searches for the reason behind this compassion, is taught about the Cross, about Jesus, about the new life awaiting her. She is converted. Words and works!

Roger Forster (Ichthus Fellowship, London) refers in lectures to the great need for this generation of Christians to accept the validity of wonders as the third corollary of evangelism. The entire book of John is built upon the fact that the signs performed by Jesus documented His deity. Should we expect such evidences today? The evangelical world is sharply split asunder over the answer to this question, with more heat than fire often present in the discussions.

All but the most naive are appalled at the sideshow techniques used by some to create miracles. A recent "faith healer" with the "gift of knowledge" was made a laughingstock when a reporter documented his clairvoyance about names, addresses and physical problems which was really the result of his wife, backstage, feeding him the information through an earplug he was wearing. Elmer Gantryism always exists on the fringes, tracing its lineage back to Simon the Sorcerer in Acts.

Don't throw out the reality with the counterfeit! If you do, your faithlessness will cut you off from the mighty flow of Christ's healing, delivering power. Those who have honestly gone to the Listening Room and have then prayed with authority have experienced glorious answers to prayer and are fully aware of the impact of wonders and words mixed together. Don't shy away from wonders as you recoil from the phonies. If there were no reality, there could be no counterfeits.

It's interesting to note that in the New Testament there is never a mention of a specific person who possesses the Gift of Healing. Every reference speaks of the gifts of healings—always plural—and seems to infer that healings are God's grace gift to the body of Christ, not to special individuals in it. James tells us that the sick are to call for the elders of the church to pray for them. Does he infer that only elders have the ability to heal? Not at all. A better understanding would be that the elders, in the intimacy of the early church, would better know the root cause of the illness. Is it the result of sin, of a stronghold, or something else? Note the continuation of the passage:

Therefore confess your sins to each other and pray for each other so that you may be healed. The prayer of a righteous man is powerful and effective. • *James 5:16*

Around the globe, Cells of Christians like your Cell Group are praying with mighty power, seeing wonders added to the words and works as the Father chooses to manifest Himself. My own brother is alive today, with normal length legs and arms, as a result of God's power in healing him. Smashed in a train accident when eight years of age, every bone on the right side of his body was broken at least once. Doctors didn't touch him for several hours, concluding he would die. Prayer warriors pulled him through. Then, after many operations to set and reset bones, his physician forecast that his right leg would be one inch shorter than his left one and that he would never have full use of his right arm. Months later he examined a perfect boy! The doctor put his head in his hands, wept and confessed he had witnessed a miracle. He was easily won to Christ by my father, an example of a harvest field in which wonders are an integral part of evangelism.

LEAD YOUR FLOCK INTO OUTREACH

As previously outlined, there should be two simultaneous stages of outreach taking place at all times through your group. The first of these will be the visitation of visitors to Congregation and Celebration gatherings.

If your church has matured enough to have Congregations, you are now a vital part of a community composed of three to five Cell Groups. In it, as well as in the Celebration gatherings, people will visit. Information from the guest cards they fill out will be sent to you. It should be directed to your Cell Group members for immediate follow-up and their report passed on through you to the central record keeping system of your church.

Your Intern should be the primary guide for this team, insuring they are fully equipped through the *Touching Hearts Guidebook*. Depending on the size and scope of the church, you may sometimes have two or more families assigned in one week. Usually, there will be no more than one and sometimes two or three weeks will pass without any assignments to your group. This gives the Cell members time to follow up each contact with more than one visit, sharing the message of salvation as appropriate with seekers.

Of course, some of these visits will be to Christians. Many will be curious about the lifestyle of your church. It is important for these to be encouraged to visit a while before committing to the life of community and ministry. Experience has proven that a Cell Church like yours can face severe problems if it is too anxious to grow by including traditional Christians who "water down" the pattern you have chosen to follow.

"Reporting in" by team members should take place in every Cell Group, along with prayer for unsaved persons who have been contacted. Every member of your Cell should know the details of every unbeliever being personally contacted by individual members.

SHARE/INTEREST GROUPS: OUTREACH TO THE UNCHURCHED

Share Groups are one of the most effective means for reaching the unchurched. Few will be won by evangelistic visits, evangelistic luncheons, or Bible studies. We are dealing with disillusioned, cynical

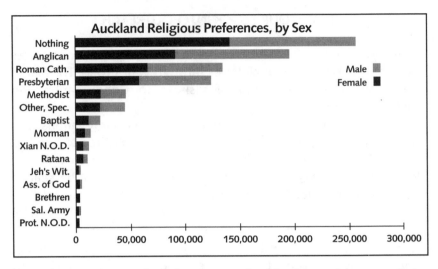

and damaged people who have already been "run over" by churches and who are not ready for another experience with them. Sadly, for years I have watched the pros in evangelism shy away from Share and Interest Groups because they begin with relationships rather than with Bible studies. When we refuse to meet the unchurched where they are and demand they meet on our terms, we are hopelessly separated from each other.

Consider the 1986 census from Auckland, New Zealand shown above. When you add those who have no church connection to the Anglicans and Roman Catholics, who are notorious for including in their body-count those who never, ever attend, the probable figure of unchurched, unreached people will be close to 65%. What would a graph of your area look like? If we are to be true to the calling of our living Lord, we must penetrate the population who are unchurched and uninterested in Christ. The actual figure of non-church attenders varies widely from city to city and nation to nation, but it always represents the majority of people.

I can assure you, from years of seeking to renew traditional churches, that in our lifetime no traditional church will sincerely seek to reach these masses! When you form Share or Interest Groups to penetrate them, you will have no competition. If we don't make them a priority, they are without a soul to love them to the Master.

The Gospel includes the good news that God has established a relationship between Himself and us. He wants to dwell in us and is ready for us to enjoy unlimited fellowship with Him. It's terribly hard to share what this relationship is all about without establishing one! Through relational *Share* or *Interest Groups*, the potential for reaching the unchurched is absolutely unlimited in comparison to present methods. They are a vital outreach of your Cell Group's ministry.

If you are a "first generation" Cell Leader, perhaps you have never attended a Share or Interest Group. You will have your hands full giving direction to these ministries, and there may not be time for you to experience them at this time. Hopefully, the second generation Cell Leaders in your church will be veterans of Share Group or Interest Group life. At the very least, you should attend some of the Share or Interest Groups and experience their dynamics.

Share and Interest Groups are specifically designed to reach out to the unchurched. A team of three meet weekly with several unchurched unbelievers. The distinction between the two types of groups is briefly shown in this illustration:

Three Fathers from a Cell Group are trained to reach out to "Type B" unbelievers. They develop a 10-week small group with them. The purpose is to develop close ties with them and their *oikos* relationships.

Each team member attaches himself or herself to two unbelievers. Since time is needed for personal times, this is a maximum "case load" for each believer. The nine people will grow close to each other through the group sessions.

The *Share Group* is developed by the selection of people from the *oikoses* of the Christians. Since these six people will not likely have anything in common, the ten weeks change topics each time the group meets. Each person in turn hosts one of the sessions and shares a topic of personal interest. Thus, one week's session might focus on a hobby of photography and the next week on how to cook gourmet dishes. The group enjoys moving from house to house and learning about what the others are interested in. The *Opening Hearts Trilogy* series of books leads the team through the ministry.

The *Interest Group* is organized in the same way, but targets people who are not known to the team members. The Cell Group might select a nearby community without any known Christians for this project. A search is made by advertising for people interested in certain topics. For example, the group might be for those wanting to learn to play a guitar or for those recovering from a divorce. The equipping module for this follows the *Opening Hearts Trilogy*, and guides the already experienced *Share Group* Team as they make contacts and form the 10-week group.

Either type of group meets when it is most convenient. Both move from house to house, including the homes of unbelievers.

THE FIVE LEVELS OF UNBELIEF

This pyramid is used in the equipping modules to explain the five levels of unbelief found among unbelievers. A pyramid is used to point out that there are always more people at the lower levels than the upper ones.

NO AWARENESS OF THE GOSPEL is the lowest level. At this stage, an unbeliever simply has no knowledge of God's desire to have a personal relationship with us. God is seen as an impersonal

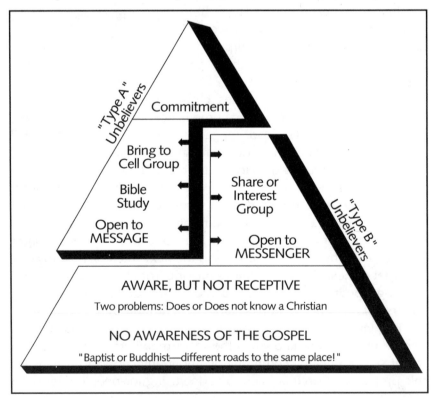

power, who can be related to by any religious view. Eastern mysticism, Christianity, other world religions are seen as being equal. They are all "ladders to God." Sadly, most of those who believe this have opted not to climb any of them. The most powerful impact on such a life is a clearly described account of your own conversion and your daily experience of personally relating to God.

AWARE, BUT NOT RECEPTIVE is the next level. Usually this person will be reachable only through the creation of a personal friendship by a committed Christian. Sometimes this will be the very first time such a contact has existed for the unbeliever. In other lives, the relationship is needed to counteract bad impressions left by other Christians.

BODY STUDY is the last level for "Type B" unbelievers. This person is not prepared to enter into Bible study. However, previous cultivation has opened the door for a Share Group experience. In this setting, topics relate to the "sting of sin" in a most tactful way and Christians are free to share their faith and walk with Christ. Note that the diagram has an open dotted line between "Body Study" and the next level, "Bible Study." As the unbeliever is impacted by the lifestyle of believers, the Holy Spirit opens the way for the Word to be valued. One-to-one study of the scriptures usually takes place first, followed by a later introduction of the seeker to the Cell Group. At this time, attendance at Celebrations and appropriate Congregation meetings can take place.

BIBLE STUDY, the first of the "Type A" levels, is a period when basic truths which lead to a personal commitment are presented. This person is on the move toward the Cross and must be lovingly led to develop a biblical understanding of God's nature, man's situation, sin, the meaning of Calvary, etc.

COMMITMENT is that period of desire leading to a conversion experience. At this final stage, the missing pieces of biblical truths are added to the concepts already grasped in the previous stage. As the person is fully aware of what it means to become a Christian, the invitation to do so is given and the decision is made—one way or the other.

Personal relationships with unbelievers at these various levels will do more to mature your flock than all the training courses in the world! Guide all your group into the appropriate ministry and encourage them as they reach out to the lost. You yourself need to be in the middle of this, developing your own contacts with unbelievers and bringing them to Christ. (Wouldn't it be absurd for you to model a Shepherd's life which has become so busy flock-tending that you have lost contact with unbelievers?)

SPONSOR REGULAR EVENTS FOR OUTREACH

The creative Shepherd will find many ways to relate the flock to those who are being cultivated. Surprise birthday parties for unbelievers, holiday parties or meals, weekend camp-outs, a day at the beach, etc., are natural ways for such relationships to be developed.

Years ago, Ruthie and I lived in Dallas. We were the only Christians on our block. For many months we were passing acquaintances of those who lived around us. We were too heavily involved in Christian activities to give them much time! (That's the very reason traditional churches will never be effective in reaching the lost.) Finally, we bolted from being captives of the system. We invited each of the neighbors over for a cup of coffee and began to spend time talking with them at the neighborhood swimming pool as our kids splashed each other.

Finally, we had a block party in our backyard. Everyone brought a couple of dishes of food, and we had a great time together. Ruth and I had, by this time, learned much about the "sin-stings" in these homes and were praying earnestly for further openings.

Across the street was a house we humorously dubbed the "Playboy Mansion." In it lived two Yuppies who threw some really noisy parties. We had tried to get a finger on their spiritual pulses, but were unable to do so. After the block party, this young couple decided to invite the neighborhood over for cocktails on a Sunday night. We got the beautifully written invitation and shuddered. What should we do? Skip church and go to a cocktail party? Whew!

In the Listening Room, we got our marching orders to accept the offer, and so we went. To our relief, the couple had anticipated we would not want whiskey and soda and tactfully offered us a choice of coke, coffee, or orange juice. There we sat, all drinking and visiting, having a great time. Then our host turned to his wife and said, "Go ahead. I know you are dying to ask Ralph your question." The lovely woman said, "Okay. I have never been to a church in my life, so this may sound stupid. But I really want to know: what is God like? Do you know how to explain Him so I can understand?"

As we realized we needed Bibles, I excused myself and ran across the street to my study. I grabbed every version and every family Bible in sight and returned with an armload. We sat there with our neighbors until midnight talking about the Word. Within six months, several couples had become committed Christians, and the lady next door had sponsored a cassette tape led Bible study for a dozen women.

As your flock develops relationships in a similar way, there will be some natural events which you should sponsor to create bridges between the group and those being cultivated. What you do and how you do it will vary from group to group—but such interactions are critical to the harvest.

HALF NIGHTS OF PRAYER BRING POWERFUL RESULTS

We shall never forget the early days at West Memorial in Houston when we would meet at the Capps' home for half nights of prayer for the lost. Not only did we experience the presence of the Holy Spirit in a special way, but we also learned as a group how to use the weapon of prayer warfare.

A weekend visit to Ichthus Fellowship in London gave me opportunity to attend such a prayer session. We sang praise songs, and the Lord became very real in our midst. Then, one by one, people shared their prayer concerns for unsaved persons they had been cultivating. A new Congregation in the area of Woolwich occupied our attention. This area of London had been the site of weapon manufacturing for centuries. All the muskets and balls used by both sides in the Battle of Waterloo came from the same buildings located there! We prayed fervently for the territory of Woolwich, which had for so long been useful to Satan in destroying lives. But the focus was on three very, very lost women who lived there. Their stories would make a statue weep. My little group of five wept as we prayed for these dear ones. Although we had never met them, we shared the burden of the woman who voiced their need to us.

You can imagine the shouts of joy at Ichthus House, where I was staying, when a telephone call reported that one of the women had given her life to Christ in the Woolwich gathering that morning! Any church can be a church of prayer—but we need to be a church of answered prayer! The impact upon Cell Group members who see their prayers answered is great. Their ministries are changed when they see answers to prayers.

Sponsor half nights of prayer as the Spirit guides you to do so. Pray for the momentum of the Cell members, that they will continue to be fruitful in the contacts and relationships which have been developed. But don't stop there! Psalm 107:2-3 says,

> *Let the redeemed of the Lord say this—those he redeemed from the hand of the foe, those he gathered from the lands, from east and west, from north and south.*

Take a period to pray for the work of Christ around the world. Lead the group to stand facing each compass point. As they all face north, ask for prayer concerns related to those who live in that direction. I am truly blessed by adopting the Korean custom of simultaneous praying out loud when such intercession is shared. There is a special fellowship in mutual prayer of this nature. Face east, south, west, each time repeating the procedure. The point is this: keep the world in focus for your flock, not just your own ministries.

Only stagnation and spiritual bankruptcy can keep your Cell Group from growing! It will multiply, as we have said repeatedly, in about six to nine months of time. As it does, Satan's domain has been penetrated and Christ has claimed His rightful ownership once again. As Abraham Kuyper wrote, "There is no sphere of life on earth over which Christ does not say, 'MINE!'"

11

Caring: A Work of Tender Love

In this chapter, I deliberately avoid using the word "counseling." Unless you have been trained in that area, you don't qualify as one, and you shouldn't think of yourself as one. Much harm can be done by novices who play around with counseling. Leave it for those who have both the spiritual and professional capacities to help deeply troubled people. Feel free to make referrals to counselors as needs within the flock become obvious to you. Always, always refer to counselors who are known by your pastoral team to practice counseling Christianly; there are Christians who use purely secular approaches, who never pray with a person and who do not discern the spiritual dynamics behind many problems.

Instead, we are going to talk about you as a caring person. Yours is a Spirit-controlled ministry dealing more with things of the spirit of man rather than emotional categories alone. Since almost all emotional problems have their roots in the spirit of a person, you will seek to focus in that area.

Consider this scripture:

The Spirit searches all things, even the deep things of God. For who among men knows the thoughts of a man except the man's spirit within him? In the same way no one knows the thoughts of God except the Spirit of God. We have not received the spirit of the world but the Spirit who is from God, that we may understand what God has freely given us. This is what we speak, not in words taught us by human wisdom but in words taught by the Spirit, expressing spiritual truths in spiritual words. •1 Corinthians 2:10-13

As you minister to those who have special needs and problems, focus not only on the circumstances which are discussed, but the spiritual source of the situation. Often we open ourselves to be invaded by the thoughts of Satan and allow ourselves to be trapped in a situation without seeing its source. To become embroiled in solving a problem without establishing the source of it is to be caught in Satan's trap! Therefore, it is important for you to secure the details of the situation and then retire to the Listening Room and listen to the Spirit, who "knows the thoughts of God." Like Paul, you can also speak words taught by the Spirit. The most important thing to discern when caring for a flock member are the strongholds which have gone unchallenged in his or her life. Until they are dealt with, problem solving is like pouring a bucket of water on a three-alarm blaze!

Consider James 1:16-17:

Don't be deceived, my dear brothers. Every good and perfect gift is from above, coming down from the Father of the heavenly lights, who does not change like shifting shadows.

The "gift" referred to here does not come wrapped in a box tied with ribbons. Rather, the word is referring to circumstances, feelings, or situations which we permit to enter our lives and control us. Gifts from above include joy, peace, kindness, faithfulness and self-control. This verse implies there are gifts that come to us which may not be from above. Therefore, when a circumstance comes to us as a "gift," we first need to question its source: is this from God?

A great danger arises when we accept gifts God may not want us to receive. Such gifts are dangerous. They may affect our mind or our physical health. Satan is a sneak: he sneaks up behind us, slips into our subconscious mind and plants fear and doubt in us. Soon these seeds sprout, and we begin to fertilize them. Perhaps we are alone in our car, driving along and this seed thought germinates. It pops into our consciousness, and we look around the car . . . no one else is present. We conclude that thought is our personal property, and so we fertilize it. Soon it grows to be a massive weed, filling the mind and overflowing into our actions. It causes mayhem in our relationships with those around us. Our life moves into crisis. We then seek help with how to handle a "bad situation," when all the time the root of the circumstance is a seed implanted in us by Beelzebub!

In Jeremiah 29:11-14a, God gives us a special word:

> " . . . For I know the plans I have for you," declares the Lord, "plans to prosper you and not to harm you, plans to give you hope and a future. Then you will call upon me and come and pray to me and I will listen to you. You will seek me and find me when you seek me with all your heart. I will be found by you," declares the Lord, "and will bring you back from captivity [Or, "and will restore your fortunes]."

Take each problem and take the person with the problem to the throne of Grace. Dig up and uncover the spiritual roots of it and the results will amaze you!

World Evangelization Crusade (WEC) is an unusual missionary society. Instead of creating a Board of Directors made up of wealthy businessmen, its founder, C. T. Studd, appointed the missionaries who were furloughing in London to serve as the mission's executive body. (He was tired of men who weren't paying the price, but managing those who were.)

In the early days, these missionaries grappled with field problems. For example, two missionary couples working in the same African town were at each other's throats. (If you can't envision that happening to missionaries, you are indeed naive!) The men wrestled for hours with the problem. On occasions, they would solve the difficulty by transferring one couple to another mission station. This did not seem to solve anything and strife would continue.

Finally, one of the men said, "We're going about this all wrong. Let's retire to our Listening Rooms and get a word from the Lord." They agreed to do so and to bring back to the Board Room a solution which would bring the greatest glory to God—regardless of how impossible it might seem for that condition to actually take place.

They returned to share what the Lord had told them. They agreed to claim by faith that His solution would become reality. With joy, they discovered God answered their prayers with solutions which seemed impossible. Missionaries wrote to tell how God had crushed the seeds of resentment that had become weeds separating them. In all the years that have followed, WEC has followed this procedure. Try it: you'll like it!

As you minister to your Cell Members, seek to discover what has been unwittingly welcomed into the life by a person. Not all "gifts" come from above! Most Christians have never learned to discern the sources of their thoughts and situations. Strongholds allow Satan to wreck lives of Christians.

When I was nine, my Dad sat in the living room of my grandfather's home and taught me to memorize Philippians 4:6-8. His gentle, fatherly direction to this scripture has guided me for over half a century:

Do not be anxious about anything, but in everything, by prayer and petition, with thanksgiving, present your requests to God. And the peace of God, which transcends all understanding, will guard your hearts and your minds in Christ Jesus. Finally, brothers, whatever is true, whatever is noble, whatever is right, whatever is pure, whatever is lovely, whatever is admirable—if anything is excellent or praiseworthy—think about such things.

Often I have had a black thought sprout, to be immediately challenged by asking: "Thought, where did you come from? Are you true? Are you noble? Are you right? Are you pure, lovely, praiseworthy? Nope! I know your source: you have been provided by the father of all lies. Since you are not from my Father, I'm going to squash you like a bug. Begone!"

Use this approach when caring for your flock. Spiritual victory will not only solve a problem, but mature a Christian. Paul Billheimer once said to me, "Most preachers run around getting their shoes singed stamping out church fires. They could solve most of them by using their knees instead!"

THE "IMPOSSIBLE" PERSONALITY

Everywhere I go, I bump into churches with Cell Groups who just "pass around" people who have "impossible" personalities. I have had my share of working with them, too. One tactless description of them is that they are "Nerds." They don't have any social sensitivity. They dominate a group session. They say tactless things, sometimes offending others. I recall one dear soul who went up to a young mother-to-be and said, "It's about time you got pregnant! You've been married for five years." Another one put on a really spiritual act in front of the group, but his children arrived with heavy bruises inflicted by his belt and his fists. One old man who was hard of hearing used to drive the group crazy by constantly reminiscing about things in his past, taking ten minutes each time to tell us a story we weren't interested in hearing.

We disgrace the power of God when we just put up with these folks, passing them on to someone else as the group multiplies. Be a caring person and cause these children of the Kingdom to grow out of the disorders which plague them. Be assured they feel miserable inside! While they probably can't put their finger on the source of their problems, they do feel they are not like other folks and wish they could be different.

There are times when it is best to work with these people for a while in private. You and your Intern, for example, might sit down with the person who is overtalking and frankly discuss the issue. If it is done in love and after praying together, the person will realize you desire to help, not to scold.

In the case of the tactless remark to the pregnant mother, the situation took place at the coffee pot, prior to the beginning of the group session. The young mother was furious! The Shepherd, aware of this, brought the issue before the entire group. It became the topic for the evening. There were two situations to work through: the woman's anger (why did she take offense?) and the insensitivity of the remark. As you can imagine, an hour and a half flew by as each person dealt with similar traits in their own lives. The tactless person was sensitized by the intensity of the situation, and it left a permanent change in his life.

The same group involvement was used to confront the father who beat up his kids. In the discussion with the man, the flock discovered he had been raised by a father who was an old German soldier, a strict disciplinarian who often brutally punished his son and who had never shown him an ounce of love. In recent months, after working for his Dad in a family business which was to be given to him, the father suddenly sold out to a stranger, pocketed the cash and left his son jobless! As his anguish over this treatment was revealed to the group, they were able to help him realize the stronghold of inner bitterness and rage, which caused him to beat his children.

Don't forward the "impossible people" to another Cell Group! Take them to the Lord and believe that all things are possible with God. They, too, can be set free from bondage and strongholds.

THE SHORT-TERM CRISIS SITUATION

Every person and every family will come to unusual times of stress or illness. There will be seasons when you will be privileged to walk into a valley with someone in your flock. Caring at such times takes on a special dimension. Death, loss of a job, serious illness, a car wreck . . . the list of such events is large.

In these times, be aware of the stages people go through:

1. Shock and Disbelief

On a sultry Sunday afternoon, her mother collapsed and died on the floor of the den. She called me, and I rushed over. Her first words were, "Why? Why did my mother die like this? We didn't even have time to say 'Goodbye' to each other!" She waited for me to answer her; instead, I just hugged her, and we cried together as we waited for the police and a funeral director to arrive. It wasn't the time to talk. It was the time to care in a nonverbal way. Later, she told me she could not remember a single thing said to her during that initial period of shock. In these situations, just hug!

2. Decision Making is Limited to Survival Conditions

"He just stuck the cigar in his mouth and walked out without saying a word. Just like he had done for thirty-five years, he just . . . went to work. And he never came home. It was three days before I discovered he had been having an affair for months."

Many new converts may arrive in your flock with variations of this story. If it has just happened, the person is unable to do anything beyond making survival decisions. This, too, is not the time for deep reflecting on the future and the lessons to be learned. For this person, caring is a matter of listening, drawing out possibilities to solve immediate problems and tactfully pointing to the ones which will bring the greatest glory to God.

Sometimes in this situation the person is rebounding with rash decisions which may enlarge the crisis. For example, one lovely young woman was so angry at discovering her husband was having an affair that she did something she had never done in her entire life. She went to a bar, met and bedded with a total stranger and became pregnant as the result. Sadly, she had no Shepherd in those days to help her handle her hurt. Her decision-making mechanism, which functioned perfectly both before and after the crisis, had broken down. A caring relationship would have protected her.

3. Learning From the Experience

Days or weeks later, there can be a time for the Shepherd to talk reflectively with persons in these situations. Discussing the experience after the pain has subsided can lead to an understanding of its impact, and new truth can be discovered. Cell Group meetings are valuable for this. In the midst of a discussion, a person may suddenly grasp new truths about an old wound.

Example: She came to our group after losing her husband by an unexpected heart attack. It was another situation where death was not kind enough to let the loved ones say farewell. Her son told me she never shed a tear during the days leading up to the burial of his body. She explained to me she didn't weep because she had to be strong for the children's sake.

Several years later, in a small group session, she shared her confusion over deciding to remarry. A fine Christian widower had proposed to her. She loved him, but could not decide to accept. Our group lovingly asked her if she had ever really buried her husband? After a long silence, she admitted in her mind he was still alive. We helped her see the reason for her problem: in her mind, remarrying would be adultery!

In an evening none of us present will ever forget, I asked her to sit on the floor with me in the middle of the group. "Imagine your husband's casket is right here. We are about to close the lid and put him in the earth. What do you want to say to him?"

She gushed tears which flowed from her deepest soul! As we all wept with her, she said tender, loving farewells to her dead husband.

When she had finished (who remembered how long it took?), I said, "Now, you take that end of the lid of this imaginary casket, and I will take this end. We'll close it together, and I will pray for God's blessing to be with you as we walk away."

Eight weeks from that night, she was married and has lived happily for years with her new husband. For her, learning from her experience took several years.

THE LONG-TERM CHRONIC SITUATION

She had been ridiculed as a child by her parents. She married at sixteen to get away from a miserable home-life. At nineteen, she was divorced with a child to care for. She went back to school, got a degree and became an excellent high school teacher. When asked about her church connections, she proudly said, "I am an agnostic. I have no religion."

Reached through a loving member of a Share Group, she finally made a decision to become a Christian. By this time, her daughter had become a hell-raising teenager. She was drawn to the Lord through the stress of the problem. She had not married again, lacking the capacity to be transparent and intimate with anyone.

Her life in the group went through a process of changing from a silent listener to a cynical commentator. As the weeks went by, she became silent again, emerging as a question-asker. Finally, after many weeks, she began to open herself to the group and to the Lord. She entered a time of throwing out garbage and inviting the Holy Spirit to renew her spirit. It was a lovely thing to watch.

You will discover that the long-term chronic will grow through several "seasons of the soul," and it can't be hurried along. Solomon's wisdom in Ecclesiastes 3 says,

> There is a time for everything and a season for every activity under heaven . . . a time to heal, a time to tear down and a time to build . . . a time to search and a time to give up, a time to keep and a time to throw away, a time to tear and a time to mend . . .

So it is with chronics who are healed. They experience what you, yourself, have learned: the Holy Spirit makes the deaf to hear according to His own timetable. Let Him hold the stopwatch; don't try to pick the time and place for someone to get their act together.

The little guy became impatient with the roses. Using a pair of scissors, he split each bud from its tip to its base. After being spanked for it, he tearfully said, "Mummy, I was just trying to help God make His roses bloom!" Don't do that with people. Some individuals have years of history to be changed, and it may take some months for the Spirit to nourish them to new life. Be patient!

DISCERNING THE IMPACT OF STRESS

Every person lives with cumulative stresses which impact their emotional stability. The Holmes-Rahe Stress Scale, the source of the table below, assesses the influence of stress. It's important to know

STRESS EVENT	VALUE	STRESS EVENT	VALUE
Death of Spouse	100	Son or Daughter	
Divorce	73	Leaving Home	29
Marital Separation	65	Trouble with In-Laws	29
Jail Term	63	Outstanding Achievement	28
Death of a Close		Spouse Begins or	
Family Member	63	Starts Working	26
Personal Injury, Illness	53	Starting or Finishing School	26
Marriage	50	Change in Living Conditions	25
Fired from Work	47	Revision of Personal Habits	24
Marriage Reconciliation	45	Trouble with Boss	23
Retirement	45	Change in Work	
Health Change in		Hours or Conditions	20
Family Member	44	Change in Residence	20
Pregnancy	40	Change in Schools	20
Sexual Difficulties	39	Change in Recreational Habits	19
Change in Social Activities	18	Change in Church Activities	19
Mortgage or loan		Addition to Family	39
under $10,000	18	Change in Sleeping Habits	16
Business readjustment	39	Change in Financial Status	38
Death of a Close Friend	37	Change in Eating Habits	15
Change in Marital Arguments	35	Change in Number	
Mortgage or Loan		of Family Gatherings	15
Over $10,000	31	Vacation	13
Christmas Season	12	Minor Violations of the Law	11
Foreclosure, Mortgage		Change in Work	
or Loan	30	Hours or Conditions	20

that each stress level is added to others, causing a total stress count which may be truly shocking. Two or three stress events which pile upon each other in the course of a year's time can bring massive changes to a personality.

Tests show that persons with severe stress are more susceptible to serious illness and have abnormally high incidences of colds, flu, etc. The spiritual life of the person is also impacted!

As you look over this list, circle the ones which are present in your life at this time. Then add all Stress Value numbers together to get your combined total. Levels of one hundred or more are frequently found. When stress factors climb high, the person functions in an entirely different manner than he or she would under less stress conditions. In fact, each of us have two ways of dealing with situations: the "normal" way and the pattern which takes over under great stress.

A fine Christian, a Godly person, had all of the following things happen in a four month period:

· Her father was killed in a plane crash.
· She was diagnosed as having breast cancer.
· Her husband lost his job.
· Her family had to move from their home to an apartment.
· Her husband had to commute to a city 200 miles away to get work and came home on weekends.

Add up the stress points in her life!

If it had not been for the strong support of a Cell Group, her marriage would have crumbled. As it was, it was spared this fate by the very slimmest of margins. Parents who lose a teenager through suicide have a very high rate of divorce. Stress crumbles their lives, and they fall apart.

You will note that one of the factors you are to record on your prayer list for each person is the stress level in their life. Prayerfully seek guidance from the Lord about what you can do to minister to those who are suffering from this malady. As you do, Paul's comment in Romans 8 will live for you:

We know that the whole creation has been groaning as in the pains of childbirth right up to the present time. Not only so, but we ourselves, who have the firstfruits of the Spirit, groan inwardly as we wait eagerly for our adoption as sons, the redemption of our bodies . . . In the same way, the Spirit helps us in our weakness. We do not know what we ought to pray for, but the Spirit himself intercedes for us with groans that words cannot express. And he who searches our hearts knows the mind of the Spirit, because the Spirit intercedes for the saints in accordance with God's will.

A WORD OF LOVING ADVICE . . .

One caution must be given before this chapter ends. Those who have done a lot of counseling are keenly aware of a condition called "transference." It's a deadly thing. It happens when a caring person becomes the object of fantasies by the person being cared for and can quickly lead to an affair. Many pastors have lost their ministries through such entanglements. It can happen to you! Your own moral integrity must be strong enough to deal with such situations when they arise.

There are a couple of simple rules for you to follow here. First of all, if you realize transference is taking place in the life of someone you are caring for, discuss it openly. Ask if these feelings you are sensing are true. If they are, help the person realize the fantasy nature of the situation, and firmly state that you would like to shift the caring relationship to your Intern, or at least include the Intern in further dialogues.

The second rule relates to your own feelings. Transference can occur within you and be unknown to the other person. Should that occur, talk it out openly with someone close to you—your spouse or a member of the Ministry Team. Don't let it go on, even if it means shifting the relationship with the person to your Intern. If you have had moral lapses in the past, protect yourself by never counseling someone of the opposite sex alone. If you are married and your spouse is appropriate for this situation, include him or her in such sessions. By all means, protect yourself from Satan's determination to devour you and your ministry. He will always be looking for your vulnerable spots, using any entrapment he can think of to end your effectiveness. Think of the devastating consequences in the lives of your flock if you fail your Lord and them through such a lapse. Don't play with fire!

If Paul, at his level of spiritual maturity, should tremble at the possibility that he could still become a castaway from his ministry by a default, don't think for a moment you are bullet-proof. Sexual involvements are devastating the witness of Christ in our generation. In the name of the Christ who promises that no temptation will overtake you that you cannot overcome, I plead with you to protect yourself from such a sordid end. Your close and transparent life with your spouse and your dearest friends are your best protection.

12

Will the Little Children Suffer?

No, I'm not misquoting the King James Bible: I'm suggesting that the little children are often made to suffer in small groups, given a clear impression they are under foot, barely tolerated, or even worse—left at home with a baby sitter.

We're going to make some fine atheists out of our children if we drag them to Cell Group gatherings. I can just imagine some man in 2021 A.D. bitterly saying, "My parents jammed that Cell Group stuff down my throat like castor oil when I was a kid. Hell will freeze over with ice before you catch me in one of 'em!"

I have shuddered many times at a remark I have heard Christian mothers make: "No, I don't want to work with kids during Cell Group time. When I come to the group, I want to have some freedom from kids. This time belongs to me. I have to take care of them all week. I want someone else to take care of them when the group meets."

It's not surprising that a young mother can feel that way. When we visit my son, I watch my daughter-in-law (with a Master's degree!) endlessly monitor the antics of her two preschoolers. Only during their nap time does she get any relief from their incessant need to be monitored. While the situation between a mother and her kids may be a classic example of familiarity breeding exhaustion, there is another side to the issue. If our children are made to feel like unwanted objects when the Cell Group meets, what will their relationship with Jesus become?

Ours is an age when too many Christians want to push off the spiritual development of their kids onto the church, in much the same way they pass along their academic development to the public schools. When shopping for a church, couples often select the one with the best program for their children. Then, without batting an eye, they will shift again when the kiddos get to an age where another church offers a better teenage program or a more dynamic youth worker. If the little darlings then turn as spiritually sour as a three day old diaper, they blame the church and drop out entirely.

No one in the world can substitute for parents where the spiritual development of children is concerned! You can't pass off personal faith as a lesson to be taught in a Sunday School class. It's not taught; it's caught. The place it is caught is at home, by parents. God meant for every child to have the insulation and security of parents and the extended family as protection from the wretchedness of a self-centered society. As long as children are in the home, there is no time or place where parents can sever themselves from them.

Thus, when a Cell Group is formed, and there are children in the family units, the spiritual extended family must give children a very special place. Cells must carefully consider how they will include children in the lifestyle of the flock.

While staying at Ichthus House in London, one of the unmarried home group members said to me, "I've got a very important meeting tonight. Some of us in the home group are going to plan for the children's activities for the next few weeks." I was impressed! Prayerfully and carefully planned activities will make strong Christians from little tots.

THE PLACE OF CHILDREN IN THE KINGDOM*

People were bringing little children to Jesus to have him touch them, but the disciples rebuked them. When Jesus saw this, he was indignant. He said to them, "Let the little children come to me and do not hinder them, for the kingdom of God belongs to such as these. I tell you the truth, anyone who will not receive the kingdom of God like a little child will never enter it." And he took the children in his arms, put his hands on them and blessed them. •Mark 10:13-16

A child has a very special relationship to the Kingdom of Heaven. It belongs to him. All little children are going to heaven. In this passage, Jesus is saying, "If you are like this little child, you, too, will be in it." That's a powerful way to test where you belong, isn't it?

Heaven belongs to the children. They have not yet learned to reject the One who gave them life. With all their lack of knowledge, they possess wisdom in spiritual matters. Rather than setting them aside when things of the Spirit are the focus, they should be honored as special envoys of truth.

At that time Jesus said, "I praise you, Father, Lord of heaven and earth, because you have hidden these things from the wise and learned and revealed them to little children. Yes, Father, for this was your good pleasure." •Matthew 11:25-26

In your Cell Group, honor childlike faith by strengthening it. Our message to children should begin by telling them the good news that the Kingdom of Heaven already belongs to them and Jesus welcomes them to choose it as their permanent possession by inviting Him to be their King. That is what it means to evangelize children: to give them the good news that they can retain what already belongs to them through the cross of Jesus and the love of God.

It's a privilege to be involved in evangelizing children in this manner. Children are the point where man and heaven meet. Where children are, heaven touches earth in a special way.

What should we teach the children in our flock meetings? First, that their permanent possession of the Kingdom of Heaven depends on his or her own decision. Think through the implications of this:

1. When a child, heaven belongs to you.
2. Unless you continue in the attitude of a child, it doesn't belong to you any more.

---

* Heartfelt thanks to Roger Mitchell of Ichthus Fellowship, London, for letting me steal his lectures to the NETWORK Interns. The final writing is mine, but the concepts are all from Him, through him.

The reason so many children do not make a decision to follow Christ as adults is simply that they never had a proper explanation in the first place. They haven't a clue about what the Kingdom of Heaven really would mean to them. So, they reject feeble religion or bad versions of Jesus. Therefore, we must show them the lifestyle of the Kingdom of Heaven—and that's what happens in a properly ordered Cell Group!

THREE CRUCIAL FACTORS

Roger Mitchell says that a child who properly experiences the Kingdom of Heaven before making an adult decision should experience three things:

1. Parents must model Kingdom relationships.

> *And He answered and said, "Have you not read, that He who created them from the beginning made them male and female and said 'For this cause a man shall leave his father and mother and shall cleave to his wife; and the two shall become one flesh'? Consequently, they are no longer two, but one flesh. What therefore God has joined together, let no man separate."* •Matthew 19:4-6

To undertake the modeling of life in the Kingdom, you need a man and a woman, united in the spiritual completeness of the marriage union. The child is the product of their physical unity, but should also be the product of their relationship to the Father.

The youngster is to understand the nature of God by seeing His attributes lived out by his parents. They are to be models before him, revealing Jehovah as a compassionate Father, as Love, as the Healer, as Provider, as Unchanging, etc. Through observing them and experiencing a loving relationship with them, the child learns the nature of God and values life spent in fellowship with Him in the Kingdom,

What happens when children grow up in the home of unsaved parents, or parents whose lifestyle endorses sin? The child, unaware of original sin and its universality, is deceived! He doesn't know the human race is fallen. Sinning parents' actions pass on the lie of Satan that all men are righteous, and it is accepted as truth by the child. All a child has to do to be deceived is to watch a fallen lifestyle modeled by parents! Since the Kingdom is seen as valueless, the child will reject it when reaching the age of accountability.

The opposite is also true. Did you know that Ruth Graham, wife of Billy Graham, has no knowledge of the exact time and place she became a Christian? Imagine! Her husband travels the earth calling men to come forward and receive Christ and his own wife never did.

No problem! Ruth was raised by Godly missionary parents in China, who tirelessly modeled life in the Kingdom for her. Stepping from the childhood possession of the Kingdom to her adult commitment was so simple, no trauma occurred. How lovely!

2. The Church must model Kingdom life

It is most significant that Paul stressed that a bride and groom are symbols of Christ and the Church:

> For the husband is the head of the wife as Christ is the head of the church, his body, of which he is the Savior. Now as the church submits to Christ, so also wives should submit to their husbands in everything. Husbands, love your wives, just as Christ loved the church and gave himself up for her to make her holy, cleansing her by the washing with water through the word and to present her to himself as a radiant church, without stain or wrinkle or any other blemish, but holy and blameless . . . This is a profound mystery—but I am talking about Christ and the church. •Ephesians 5:23-27, 32

Here's where your Cell Group comes in! You are the spiritual family of the Kingdom for the children in your midst. In a society where the majority of children are not raised by their true parents—and where many a child is raised by a single parent—the importance of the group is magnified tenfold. Here, then, is an extended family for children of broken homes. Every child must be properly received.

> He took a little child and had him stand among them. Taking him in his arms, he said to them, "Whoever welcomes one of these little children in my name welcomes me; and whoever welcomes me does not welcome me but the one who sent me." •Mark 9:36-37

We are to actually receive each child into the group as though we were welcoming Jesus Himself into our midst! This makes our relationship to each child very, very special.

In Auckland, I visited one of the home groups of the Hillsborough Baptist Church. We had about seven children in our midst. I asked them to sit in a circle, facing out. Then the adults sat on the floor facing a child and told them stories about their lives when they were the age of the child. The ten-year-old I talked to was immediately bonded to me, and we had a great time together for the rest of the evening.

Such bonding between every adult with every child is very important. Becoming "Uncle Ralph" to children is something I started years ago in our very first home Cell Group meetings. From time to time, one of those youngsters, now an adult, will call and say, "Uncle Ralph, I've got to talk to you!" As we struggle with current crises, I remember earlier times when they were children, and we rode down a roller coaster staring into each other's eyes, waiting for the other person to "chicken out" as we swooped down the track. Or, the times when we took a trip together to the ice cream parlor. Or, when we competed in ball games at TOUCH Ranch against their parents, or walks along the beach, or spooky stories I told in the dark during retreats. All these events bonded us to each other in ways that brought us back together later.

It doesn't stop with fun times, however! Praying with Lyle Jessup when I was fourteen years old has impacted my entire life. My, how that man laid hold on God during the prayer times when I, a teenager, was his only companion. After 51 years, I still remember how we spent a New Year's Eve praying together and how our Lord manifested Himself to us.

Make those children a vital part of your group life. During times when you are going to have "grown up talk," deliberately rotate each of the adult members to spend quality time with the children. Plan what you will do. There are excellent videotapes available which can be used to teach the Bible to them. Or, go to your nearest Christian bookstore and buy some Vacation Bible School material and use it as a source for craft work, games, songs, scripture quizzes, etc. Better yet, if one of your members has a home video camera, let the children produce a documentary on a Bible book. Let the kids dress up in costumes they make themselves and act out Paul in Ephesus, or Daniel in the den of lions, or Abraham and Isaac. Let an older child be the cameraman. When it is completed (it could take several weeks), have a special showing for the entire Cell Group.

Include the youngsters in your praise times. Teach them to pray by letting them see you pray with urgency and then lead them to pray along with you. Let them read the scripture. Have a story time for them and pass the story-telling around among all the adults. For members who aren't too creative, get children's story books (available from your Christian bookstore).

3. Communicated by the Angels

See that you do not look down on one of these little ones. For I tell you that their angels in heaven always see the face of my Father in heaven. •Matthew 18:10

Angels lobby for children before the throne of God. Every single one of us is assigned an angel at birth, and this heavenly servant is always attending us. Angels are present to protect the child, messengers to bring God's word. Angels are also "stage hands," overseeing the set as the child acts out the unsophisticated deeds which could be harmful. Angels move cars around them, deflect scissor points from eyes, keep bottle caps from being opened and poison swallowed, avoiding what would otherwise be a calamity. (Even angels have a rough time looking after kids in today's world!)

If you are a sophisticate who has swept the issue of angels under the rug, you have a moral obligation to get out your concordance and check all the references to them. You might also want to read Billy Graham's book, *Angels, Angels, Angels!* They are present, and they are a part of the Divine pattern for revealing the Kingdom to children.

Our angel doesn't abandon us when we reach puberty. Even if the "little child" is sixty-three years of age, his or her angel is still lobbying, desperately pleading before the throne of God on his or her behalf.

Thus, we see God's three part pattern for helping a child choose to remain in the Kingdom. Keeping what is deemed valuable is no contest, is it?

STUMBLING BLOCKS BRING SERIOUS CONSEQUENCES

*And whoever welcomes a little child like this in my name
welcomes me. But if anyone causes one of these little ones
who believe in me to sin, it would be better for him to have
a large millstone hung around his neck and to be drowned in
the depths of the sea. Woe to the world because of the
things that cause people to sin! Such things must come, but
woe to the man through whom they come!*

•Matthew 18:5-7

Note that the preceding verse, related to angels, is given just
after these words are spoken by Jesus. The angels are mentioned in
the context of children who are despised and who are made to
"stumble."

Stumbling blocks are low lying objects which may be unnoticed
and which cause children to fall as they walk. A child's inheritance,
the Kingdom of Heaven, is not primarily his or her responsibility. It
is the responsibility of the parents, the church and the angels, all
stewards of it. If it is afterwards stolen away because of stumbling
blocks, woe to such a person! It would be better for that person to
have never been born.

Stumbling blocks are Satan's devices. He attacks children, and
his demons seek to destroy them (See Mark 7:26-30, Luke 9:38-43).
Demons will pressure moms and dads from being the blessers of
children to becoming their accusers.

Millions of children have been robbed of their inheritance in the
Kingdom of Heaven. The sins of the fathers are visited to the third
and fourth generations. The robbery has been so great that many
children have a hard time receiving the Kingdom at all. Thus, there
is a need for healing among children who are caused to stumble and
smashed long before the age of accountability.

THE "AGE OF ACCOUNTABILITY"

When does this transition from childhood to adulthood take
place? Lots of theologians have tried to give a formula for it. Some
point to the Jewish rite of Bar Mitzvah as the "legal" age when a
child becomes an adult. Some religious educators become totally

hostile at the thought of presenting a need to accept Christ as Lord and Savior until after the age of fourteen.

The scripture doesn't say a single thing about this matter. If it were a clear cut issue, surely the Holy Spirit would have settled the matter with a statement from Jesus or Paul or someone else. Thus, we are left to conclude the answer from observation alone. I'm going to share mine, for what it's worth.

The exact age of accountability will vary from child to child. Some seem to be born with a sensitivity to spiritual things. Much depends on the atmosphere in the home. Even within the same family environment, no two are the same. From birth, there was a significant difference between Jacob and Esau. John the Baptist was unique before his birth, selected for a special task by his God. Accountability is a variable thing.

I myself was soundly, genuinely converted at the end of my fifth year, sitting on the lap of my godly father. I can still recall the profound need to receive Jesus into my life which came to me as he preached in a little chapel in Northumberland, Pennsylvania. Mother doubted my ability to grasp such truths and let Dad talk to me. I shall be forever grateful for his sensitivity and the way he brought me to personal faith.

Another child I heard about asked his father if he would pray with him to become a Christian. The father responded, "Son, you're too young." Eyes brimming with tears, the little guy said, "But Daddy, if I'm not too young to love you, why am I too young to love Jesus?" Beware of stumbling blocks!

However, there's a deeper issue than loving Jesus. It is the capacity of the child to know how sin separates us from the Father. Innocence changes to accountability when a child begins to deliberately choose to take the control of his or her life out of the hands of God.

My youngest son began to tell us he wanted to let Jesus come into his heart when he was about five years old. Each time he brought the subject up, his mother or I would say, "Do you know what 'sin' is?" "No," he would say. We would explain in child words what we meant. For weeks we repeated this scene. It would always be obvious to us that he had no awareness of sin. We rightly concluded that if you don't know you're lost, you can't be saved.

A dentist friend of ours took his family and ours on a houseboat jaunt on Lake Texoma on the Labor Day weekend when our son was six years old. We had a wonderful time swimming and fishing. The first night out we found a small sand island and commandeered it for a campfire. As we sat around the dying embers, I suggested we go around the circle and each share how we came to accept Jesus into our lives. Little Randall was sitting on my lap, wrapped in a blanket, listening intently. All the adults and children shared the witness of their conversions. When we finished Randall said firmly to the group, "I'm not a Christian." Tactfully, I said, "Would you like to be?" Very thoughtfully, he said "No."

Alone with him soon after, I asked him once again if he understood what "sin" was, and he gave me a clear-cut answer. Ruthie and I were convinced he had reached his age of accountability—and with it, he was counting of the cost of entering the Kingdom, where only Christ can be Lord. In the days that followed he was the object of special intercession. A month later, he prayed to receive Christ with his mother.

I believe the age of accountability happens like that. When a child does come to the moment of commitment, it should be a very, very special event for the Cell Group. There should be a lovely celebration equal to a Bar Mitzvah! That youngster should never, ever forget the joy in the Kingdom family over the decision to follow Jesus forever.

One group I know presents each child at that time with an expensive leather Bible, which has a small word written in the blank pages by every adult member. Imagine what memories those notes and that Bible will have for a lifetime!

WHAT CAN WE DO FOR CHILDREN?

Roger suggests the following:

1. Joyfully tell the children the good news that the Kingdom of Heaven belongs to them now.
2. Be Godly parents and help others to be so.
3. Receive children in the way Jesus received them:
   • By blessing them (Matthew 19:14).
   • By laying hands on them and praying for them (Matthew 19:15).
4. Involve them in the whole Kingdom of God (Mark 9:36). Note how Jesus put a child on his knee in the center of the disciples.

Sometimes put the children in the middle of the group. At times, center what you are doing around them. Affirm them.

5. Use them as "Agents of the Kingdom." Even as Jesus used the disciples to distribute food to the five thousand, let them do tasks in the meetings.

6. Encourage them to take a lead in worship:

> But when the chief priests and the teachers of the law saw the wonderful things he did and the children shouting in the temple area, "Hosanna to the Son of David," they were indignant. "Do you hear what these children are saying?" they asked him. "Yes," replied Jesus, "have you never read, 'From the lips of children and infants you have ordained praise'?" •Matthew 21:15-16

Each child can be led to discover how to praise, how to worship, how to lead the group in prayer, how to talk about Jesus without shyness.

7. Undo the work the enemy has already done and prevent children from tripping over stumbling blocks. The angels don't interfere in parental responsibility. If parents squeeze out the angels and expose children to the onslaught of the enemy, the angels may not be able to prevent what is happening. However, you may be sure they are lobbying at the Throne about the precise details that are taking place!

CHILDREN CAN FIND LOST SHEEP, TOO!

Being a parent of a runaway is the most painful thing a parent can experience short of the death of the child. As a Shepherd, you may meet a rebellious youngster who is taking a long time climbing up fool's hill. Our society pushes drugs, condoms and sex on children not yet teenagers. It is not possible for your flock to penetrate the domain of darkness without making contact with children whose lives are already messed up.

Your community is filled with kids who need Christ! Don't think only in terms of ministering to the children in the Cell Group. Such self-centeredness is evil and destroys an important dimension of your modeling Kingdom life before your watching children.

ABOUT TEENAGE CELL GROUPS

When my oldest son was fifteen, we spent many hours together in "Pimple Park," so nicknamed because of its many grassy mounds. It was a major transfer point for drugs among teenagers. He learned how to reach out to those his own age in that setting. Next, he discipled a young Mexican lad, who in turn went to Mexico and reached hundreds of druggies for Jesus. By the time he finished high school, he was more experienced at sharing his faith than my deacons! Lead your Cell Group members' teenage children into faith sharing.

HOW WE BEGAN OUR TEENAGE CELLS

We started Teen Age Cell Groups when we were still transitioning from being a "church with cells" to a pure Cell Church. We still had a poorly attended Sunday evening service. The only teens who came were those who were forced to attend—like my son and seven other Deacon's kids. They would sit in the back row, chew gum, and generally look bored. Something had to change!

Following a policy that Lawrence Khong has made famous, instead of looking for a *program* to solve the problem, I looked for a *leader*. His name was Jimmy Dorrell. Not only did he attend college and seminary, but he was also "street smart," which is important when you are working with teenagers.

Jim explained his policies to me: The teenagers would conduct the Cells and adults would be in the background. There would be many retreats to get kids out of their environment so they could be impacted. We should shut down the Sunday night services, he said, because that was the best time for teens to meet. (I gladly did so!)

Each teenage Cell Group sponsored a Share Group who passed out dozens of typed cards in their schools like the one shown on the next page. They also cruised around on Sunday afternoons from three p.m. until starting time, rounding up kids who were sitting in cars drinking beer in front of quick-stops and apartment swimming pools. The ministry grew rapidly, but not as fast as the spiritual growth of the Christian kids who were doing it. Not an adult was in sight when the Sunday evening sessions took place, except for those handing out food in the kitchens of the houses where they met.

Teenagers reached teenagers! Through the years of pastoring in the traditional church, I had seen a lot of "discipleship" courses for young people come and go. I never saw one which truly matured youth like Share Group training and ministry activities.

It's unusual to have three teenagers in one adult Cell Group, although it can happen. When it does, create a special Share Group using them. If you have only one or two teens, include one or two from a nearby Cell Group in your Congregation. This can also be accomplished by letting Congregations sponsor teenage Cells.

Let every youngster who is old enough to make a personal decision to accept Christ become a witness to his friends. Encourage this to be a part of your own family gatherings by inviting unsaved friends of your own children to share a meal in your home. As you complete the meal with family devotions, let your child pray in front of his or her friend. Answer questions about Jesus these children may ask you. Hold a "backyard Bible club" for them and let your own child take a major part in what takes place.

Do you begin to sense the joy, the excitement and the lasting impact your Cell Group will have on its children? Ten years from now, you will see the fruit of your labors. I have been through the cycle, and it's great!

```
            YOU ARE INVITED TO A
                GET-TOGETHER
           FOR TEENAGERS ONLY.
                TOPICS LIKE
        "HOW TO MANAGE YOUR PARENTS"
      Led by Jim Smith and Mary Martin,
      Seniors at Stratford High School
      Meets Sunday Nights, 6:30 p.m.,
        rotates from house to house.
           For information, call
             Jim at 435 6541
            Mary at 742 8894
```

Typed invitations similar to this were passed out in high schools in Houston to develop Teenage Share Groups. The Cell Groups which gathered converts from this activity grew to 100 kids in 18 months!

A FURTHER WORD ABOUT HOW
JIMMY DORRELL STARTED

He trained my son along with the Deacon's kids to be the core group. One day he came to me and said, "Randall is probably going to ask you to help him put together Sunday night's Cell Group activity. Please don't help him." He did so, and I refused. He went to his desk and began to prepare his heart as well as the activities, and was never the same again.

I watched the Cells grow. Jimmy gave them all titles taken from the Greek alphabet letters and when the number of groups exceeded them he used the Hebrew alphabet. There were many conversions through the teen Cells. There were Sundays when as many as 20 teenagers made a public profession of faith. When he reached 100 in Cells in 18 months, I knew we had crossed a new frontier in our life as a Cell Church.

Prayer became a vital part of the teenager's lives. One Tuesday morning I attended an early morning prayer meeting where a couple of hundred students were agonizing before the Lord over the spiritual needs in the lives of their parents and their friends.

The teenage Cells became so popular that for three years in a row, Jimmy was elected by the Senior class of our local high school to bring the valedictory address at graduation.

Many dramatic stories have come from that period of time— stories of girls who *didn't* get abortions, of guys who *did* kick the drug habit, of brilliant young men who heard the Lord's call into ministry and gave up thier ambitions for great careers.

The principles Jimmy laid down are important:

1. Adult leadership equips the teens and does not lead their Cells.
2. Retreats are a vital part of the equipping ministry for teens.
3. Cells should all meet at the same time, rotating between homes of students wherever possible.
4. Frequent get-togethers for all the Cells at the close of their meetings for fun and recreation are vital. (I shall never forget a Sunday night in hot July when 2 tons of snow was blown from a special truck for a snowball fight!)

Teenage Cell Groups are vital to your Cell Church life!

13

Too Much Month at the End of the Money

Cell Groups are filled with people who have electronically charged themselves into poverty. They also contain folks who have plenty of dollars and spend them as fast as they come in on whatever they want next. A smaller group are those who are both financially successful and penurious to the core, stashing far more than their share of wealth. Few Christians realize that we should live simply in order that others can simply live.

It's rare to find a Christian who has a biblical concept of stewardship. The best we see is the family who tithes faithfully and then spends the other ninety per cent on—you guessed it—whatever they want next.

While it may be rare to find a Christian value system where wealth is concerned, it's not surprising when you think about how the subject is dealt with by the traditional church. Of all its many shortcomings, the P.B.D. church can point to its curriculum on stewardship as the saddest of all.

Tithing is touted as the minimum goal for all Christians. God gets His share right off the top—before taxes, before bills, before anything. And, of course, "God" means "the local church." Its teaching on tithing is basically self-serving.

I once examined the budgets of forty Richmond, Virginia churches varying in annual size from over a million dollars to less than a hundred thousand. I was stunned to discover that not one of them spent more than two per cent of their budget for materials or classes to train or educate their memberships, and what they did spend went primarily for Sunday School literature. When their budget was divided by their reported conversions, it was not at all uncommon to discover each profession of faith cost from $20,000 to $80,000 each.

What was their money spent for? Usually, about ten per cent went to all outside missionary causes. That left ninety per cent to be spent on themselves. Thirty to fifty per cent of this went to pay off building loans, another fifteen per cent was used for utilities and to maintain the buildings, with most of the balance used to pay salaries. In all forty cases, benevolence was handled by putting men at the door to collect small dollar offerings once a month at the end of a communion service. So much for bringing good news to the poor!

Few people have ever stopped to realize that churches send more money to money lenders than will ever be sent to mission fields. With churches borrowed to the hilt, what can it say to its members who do the same?

Doesn't anyone ever ask, "Is this the way God wants His money spent?" Yes: those who have given up on the church always ask this question, over and over. But pastors who are trying to raise the annual budget and launch a "Together We Build (Again?) Campaign" are too occupied to answer their queries.

Television evangelists need more than local churches, so they offer free gifts to all who send $100—like family Bibles they buy in volume from a Nashville firm for four bucks. In addition, they offer the Great Slot Machine In The Sky, offering prosperity as the blessing for contributing. To prove their point, they force themselves to live in nine thousand square foot homes and wear Rolex watches. Our dollars will go to "spread the Gospel," we are told, which means surrendering it to the electronic men who will invest it as God directs. There are a million causes to soak up God's money, all called ways to "spread the Gospel." Ugh!

WHAT DID THE EARLY CHURCH DO WITH GOD'S MONEY?

If we objectively search the New Testament, a clear pattern of what God does with His wealth is revealed. The reason this pattern is seldom presented is because of the havoc it would play in the support of religious institutions.

1. They cared for one another.

All the believers were together and had everything in common. Selling their possessions and goods, they gave to anyone as he had need. •Acts 2:44-45

All the believers were one in heart and mind. No one claimed that any of his possessions was his own, but they shared everything they had. With great power the apostles continued to testify to the resurrection of the Lord Jesus and much grace was upon them all. There were no needy persons among them. For from time to time those who owned lands or houses sold them, brought the money from the sales and put it at the apostles' feet and it was distributed to anyone as he had need. Joseph, a Levite from Cyprus, whom the apostles called Barnabas (which means Son of Encouragement), sold a field he owned and brought the money and put it at the apostles' feet. •Acts 4:32-37

These are the first two scriptures which give us a clue about what early Christians did with their money. They helped each other! Note how they did it: It was designated through the Apostles. It's not a good idea to directly give aid to a member of the Cell Group. It should come anonymously as from the Body and not from one person to another.

The pastor of one Cell Church called the Cell Leaders together on the last Sunday of each month to discuss needs within the Cell Groups. They first paid all the bills incurred by the church. Then, they emptied the bank account by helping members and others who had serious financial needs. Thousands of dollars of checks were written in these sessions. The funds were then quietly distributed by the Cell Leaders through home visits.

Of course, there are situations where a person is not helped by such gifts! Knowing when to help financially and when to give wise counsel instead is very important. Those who do not know how to handle money will not be helped by such gifts.

2. They supported church planters.

> *Moreover, as you Philippians know, in the early days of your acquaintance with the Gospel, when I set out from Macedonia, not one church shared with me in the matter of giving and receiving, except you only; for even when I was in Thessalonica, you sent me aid again and again when I was in need. Not that I am looking for a gift, but I am looking for what may be credited to your account. I have received full payment and even more; I am amply supplied, now that I have received from Epaphroditus the gifts you sent. They are a fragrant offering, an acceptable sacrifice, pleasing to God.*
> •Philippians 4:15-18

In contrast to the church at Philippi, Paul had to deal severely with the Corinthian church. Being mixed up about the need to support church planters was only one of their many problems:

> *Who serves as a soldier at his own expense? Who plants a vineyard and does not eat of its grapes? Who tends a flock and does not drink of the milk? Do I say this merely from a human point of view? Doesn't the Law say the same thing? For it is written in the Law of Moses: "Do not muzzle an ox while it is treading out the grain." [Deut. 25:4] Is it about oxen that God is concerned? Surely he says this for us, doesn't he? Yes, this was written for us, because when the plowman plows and the thresher threshes, they ought to do so in the hope of sharing in the harvest. If we have sown spiritual seed among you, is it too much if we reap a material harvest from you? If others have this right of support from you, shouldn't we have it all the more? But we did not use this right. On the contrary, we put up with anything rather than hinder the Gospel of Christ. Don't you know that those who work in the temple get their food from the temple and those who serve at the altar share in what is offered on the altar? In the same way, the Lord has commanded that those who preach the Gospel should receive their living from the Gospel.*
> •1 Corinthians 9:7-14

Their pattern is clear to us. They cared for their own, and they cared about the transmission of the Gospel to other cities. Many Cell Churches today are more of a movement than a geographically defined Body of Christ. Faith Community Baptist Church in Singapore has church planters in many nations of the world. They consider their pastoral teams overseas as part of the church staff, not missionaries. District Pastors commute between Singapore and those outposts. The same pattern for church life is used in all areas.

Lead your Cell Group to think globally! Don't let their vision end at the edge of the neighborhood. Keep a world in view.

3. They supported new work.

> I robbed other churches by receiving support from them so as to serve you. And when I was with you and needed something, I was not a burden to anyone, for the brothers who came from Macedonia supplied what I needed. I have kept myself from being a burden to you in any way and will continue to do so. •2 Corinthians 11:8-9

Note that the money was brought to Paul! Epaphroditus was one of the delegates to deliver a support gift to Paul. He stayed on in Rome to do the work of ministry as Paul directed. So committed was he to his task he nearly died. Paul speaks lovingly of him in his Philippian letter.

It is a wonderful thing for your church to do the same. Send out a team along with the financial support gift. Share your lives as well as your money. All will be blessed by this method of support.

4. They rallied around sister congregations in distress.

> During this time some prophets came down from Jerusalem to Antioch. One of them, named Agabus, stood up and through the Spirit predicted that a severe famine would spread over the entire Roman world. (This happened during the reign of Claudius.) The disciples, each according to his ability, decided to provide help for the brothers living in Judea. •Acts 11:27-29

The need in Judea became a concern for many of the young churches in Asia. Several other scriptures refer to this fund, collected to help the dear Christians who had first been jailed and then expelled from Jerusalem and scattered throughout the province of Judea.

Note the use of God's money here. Once again, it is put into meeting the needs of people in distress, not spent for fancy buildings with pipe organs.

> Now, however, I am on my way to Jerusalem in the service of the saints there. For Macedonia and Achaia were pleased to make a contribution for the poor among the saints in Jerusalem. They were pleased to do it and indeed they owe it to them. For if the Gentiles have shared in the Jews' spiritual blessings, they owe it to the Jews to share with them their material blessings. •Romans 15:25-27

> Now about the collection for God's people: Do what I told the Galatian churches to do. On the first day of every week, each one of you should set aside a sum of money in keeping with his income, saving it up, so that when I come no collections will have to be made. Then, when I arrive, I will give letters of introduction to the men you approve and send them with your gift to Jerusalem. If it seems advisable for me to go also, they will accompany me. •1 Corinthians 16:1-4

Note the recurring pattern! Paul didn't want to get involved in fund raising. It was to be done internally. The collection was to be delivered by the Corinthians. Their love, their encouragement, was as valuable as the money which would be given to families.

> And now, brothers, we want you to know about the grace that God has given the Macedonian churches. Out of the most severe trial, their overflowing joy and their extreme poverty welled up in rich generosity. For I testify that they gave as much as they were able and even beyond their ability. Entirely on their own, they urgently pleaded with us for the privilege of sharing in this service to the saints. And they did not do as we expected, but they gave themselves first to the Lord and then to us in keeping with God's will.
> •2 Corinthians 8:1-5

That's it. According to the book of Acts and all of the Gospels, that's what they did with their money! It would be two hundred years before churches would get into the building contracting business! A rented Hall of Tyrannus is mentioned in the latter part of Acts, used for special meetings. Mostly, they used their own homes for their gatherings.

Have you ever thought about how inexpensively the church could be operated if it departed from its campus mentality? Cell Groups and Share Groups require no real estate. Quite often, lodge halls, schools, motel meeting rooms and even church buildings can be rented for Congregation meetings. The one piece of real estate Cell Churches around the world seem to build is a massive auditorium for Celebrations, prayer meetings and special events. By the time the Cells have multiplied enough to need a huge auditorium, the church is so big that they pay cash for construction. (At the time I write these words, I know of no exceptions to that statement.)

WHAT IS GOD'S PLAN OF ECONOMY?

The complete answer to that would fill a good sized book. Fortunately, it has already been written, and I highly recommend it: *God's Miraculous Plan of Economy*, by Jack R. Taylor. It belongs on your book shelf!

In addition, here are some thoughts which might be worth discussing with your flock:

1. We should have no "second source" of wealth; God is sufficient.

And God is able to make all grace abound to you, so that in all things at all times, having all that you need, you will abound in every good work. As it is written: "He has scattered abroad his gifts to the poor; his righteousness endures forever." [Psalm 112:9] Now he who supplies seed to the sower and bread for food will also supply and increase your store of seed and will enlarge the harvest of your righteousness. You will be made rich in every way so that you can be generous on every occasion and through us your generosity will result in thanksgiving to God. •2 Corinthians 9:8-11

Too many of us have for a motto, "In God We Trust—Alongside My Savings Account." Now, there's nothing wrong with savings accounts and investments. That's not the point: the issue is looking upon them as your backup system if the Lord fails to supply all your needs.

2. We should recognize our responsibility to be 100%, not 10% stewards.

> But just as you excel in everything—in faith, in speech, in knowledge, in complete earnestness and in your love for us [Some manuscripts in our love for you]—see that you also excel in this grace of giving. I am not commanding you, but I want to test the sincerity of your love by comparing it with the earnestness of others. For you know the grace of our Lord Jesus Christ, that though he was rich, yet for your sakes he became poor, so that you through his poverty might become rich. And here is my advice about what is best for you in this matter: Last year you were the first not only to give but also to have the desire to do so. Now finish the work, so that your eager willingness to do it may be matched by your completion of it, according to your means. For if the willingness is there, the gift is acceptable according to what one has, not according to what he does not have. Our desire is not that others might be relieved while you are hard pressed, but that there might be equality. At the present time your plenty will supply what they need, so that in turn their plenty will supply what you need. Then there will be equality, as it is written: "He who gathered much did not have too much and he who gathered little did not have too little." [Exodus 16:18] •2 Corinthians 8:7-15

It really grieves me to see brothers and sisters in God's family choose a life of unnecessary opulence. Explaining that they give thousands of dollars to the Lord's work, and they are entitled to live that way doesn't make spiritual sense. It's a contradiction in value systems to talk of a burden for reaching the world from your mansion's verandah. While this is a deeply personal matter, there should be sensitivity in this area among us all.

3. We should support missionaries, not missions.

Dear friend, you are faithful in what you are doing for the brothers, even though they are strangers to you. They have told the church about your love. You will do well to send them on their way in a manner worthy of God. It was for the sake of the Name that they went out, receiving no help from the pagans. We ought therefore to show hospitality to such men so that we may work together for the truth.
·3 John 1:5-8

I have been a home missionary and a foreign missionary. I have lived among missionaries. There's a whale of a difference between them, and you don't realize it until you see them on the field. I frankly say that I have met some of the most dedicated of all God's saints in foreign countries. I am thinking of men with earned doctorates who are living in the most primitive of conditions, unsparingly pouring themselves into church planting. "The world is not worthy of them!" And, sad to say, I have also met a few who are among the laziest, least productive people in God's work.

There are as many "strategies" for missions as there are mission boards, and they are not all created equal. Some missions create teams which work themselves out of an area in a few years. Others move in with hospitals, seminaries, publishing houses, television studios and build massive buildings that can never be turned over to the nationals, because they won't ever have the cash flow to pay the annual taxes on the property.

For example, in a mission meeting in Asia, the treasurer gleefully announced to the missionaries that he had held back their budget spending that year and was sending over nine hundred thousand dollars back to the home office. Knowing the policy of his mission board was to designate returned funds to buy securities against the day when support would dry up (there are tens of millions of dollars of tithes and offerings in that mission's reserves right now), I made a commitment to never, ever again just "send money" to organizations without checking them out. I urge you to do the same!

Some missionary societies have clearly focused on establishing Cell Groups as the basic building block for church planting. They are worthy of your support. As your church makes commitments to expand its ministry to other cities or countries, the New Testament pattern which supported Paul's ministry is repeated. But before you commit thousands of dollars, invest a few hundred to send someone from your church to check things out. Then, as the Lord leads, you may send out workers as well as dollars to enlarge the ministry base there. *(Who knows? One of them may be you!)*

MORE THAN ENOUGH

There will always be more than enough to do the work of the Lord if it really is His work! People who get angry when "the preacher talks about money" have other problems than financial ones. They are self-centered and don't want anyone tampering with their bad stewardship. However, in the intimacy of a Cell Group setting, with the emphasis on helping people rather than supporting institutions, there should be levels of voluntary giving that will shame traditional churches. My participation in the ministry of the Faith Community Baptist Church has been one of the greatest blessings of my life! The contributions of the Cell Group members equals a 100% tithe from each family!

Be a model in this area, and you will have boldness when discussing New Testament stewardship with the Flock.

Part Three

Shepherding
Your
Cell Group

CELL GROUP GATHERINGS CAN TAKE MANY FORMS

- AN AGAPE MEAL (4 HOURS)
  (Includes the Lord's Supper)

- A REGULAR MEETING (1 1/2 HOURS)

- A WEEKEND RETREAT

- A HALF NIGHT OF PRAYER

- A BIRTHDAY PARTY

- A LAUGH N' GIGGLE PARTY

- A GET-TOGETHER FOR UNBELIEVERS
  (Perhaps for home-made ice cream)

- A CHRISTMAS CAROLLING NIGHT

- A DAY AT THE BEACH OR MOUNTAINS

- A PRAYER WARFARE WALK

They helped every one his neighbor
and everyone said to his brother,
"Be of good courage!"
• Isaiah 41:6

14

How Cell Groups Function

And let us consider how to stimulate one another to love and good deeds, not forsaking our own assembling together, as is the habit of some, but encouraging one another; and all the more, as you see the day drawing near. •Hebrews 10:24-25

These verses, referring to the Cell Groups of the earliest church, help us understand why they met together. Their gathering was for interactive communication, not for teaching. They "stimulated one another." Perhaps the greatest blight among Christians in our day is the lack of heart-sharing and personal interaction. Cell Groups provide a setting where there can be maximum sharing, maximum encouragement of one another.

". . . to love and good deeds. . ."

The stimulation of one another is threefold:

1. To increase our love for one another.
   Authentic love comes as a process, not an event. The continual meeting times are necessary for love to become deep rooted.

2. The gatherings should increase the "good deeds" of the Cell Group members.

Sharing the Gospel with others through relationships, through "good deeds," caused the New Testament church to grow from 3,000 to 10,000 in a matter of weeks! Never, ever forget that every one of us is a minister, and every Cell Group should engage every Christian member in serving the needs of unbelievers.

" . . . but encouraging one another; and all the more, as you see the day drawing near."

3. To encourage one another.

The need for others to listen, to love, to stand beside us when we are going through the crises of life, becomes greater as we approach the end of the age! Surely that phrase should stimulate us to realize the importance of Cell Groups.

CELL GROUPS WILL GO THROUGH 4 STAGES

As your Cell Group forms, expect these four stages to be normal:

1. The Get-Acquainted Stage

Perhaps someone has said to you, "You aren't a bit like I thought you were when we first met!" This is a common reaction. First impressions are often based on past relationships with other people. It can take two or three sessions before Cell Group members overcome these false conclusions about each other. (This process can be sped up by the use of a Spiritual Formation Retreat, where you have concentrated time to spend with each other.)

2. The Conflict Stage

When people really get to know each other, value systems will clash. One person may talk too much, making the Cell Group feel angry by this unwanted domination. Another person may be insensitive; someone else may be too sensitive. After four or five sessions together, these conflicts will surface in Cell Group discussions. A "sand-papering" effect will take place. People then begin to trust each other enough to air their differences and to work through them.

If you have never been in a small group, you may find the first experience with the Conflict Stage a bit scary. Don't be afraid! Gently guide the Cell Group, letting the participants share deeply. The members WILL resolve these differences. The result is DRAMATIC! For the first time, the group's identity will be established and commitment to the Cell Group will occur.

3. The Community Stage

The Conflict stage is followed by a meaningful period in which the members grow into one another in a very special way. It is not only the period of enrichment: it is also the danger point! Because the Cell Group has found meaningful relationships, it may decide it wants to close itself off, to remain undisturbed. If this is permitted, the Cell Group will turn into an ugly, selfish monster.

4. The Ministering-to-Others Stage

In the very first meeting, emphasize that the Cell Group exists to strengthen its members to help others. At the outset, every member should be encouraged to become a part of a Visitation Team. However, some of the members will not be ready to minister to others until the Cell Group reaches this fourth stage. As soon as the Cell Group has reached Stage 3, emphasize the importance of every member being involved in enlisting others and serving needs of team members.

CELL GROUPS HAVE A SIX MONTH LIFE

Long years of experience with groups has verified that they stagnate after a certain period. People draw from one another for the first six months; after that, they tend to "coast" along together. For that reason, each Cell Group will be expected to multiply naturally after six to nine months or be restructured.

As a Cell Group Servant, you should be in the constant process of training someone else as an Intern. The greatest tribute which can be paid to you as a Cell Group Leader is for your Cell Group to double and multiply itself into two groups.

Set this as a goal and work toward that moment when your Cell Group "births" a daughter Cell Group. By the time this happens you should have fully trained your Intern to become the Cell Group Servant of this daughter Cell Group.

CELL GROUPS HAVE A TEN WEEK CYCLE

Have you noticed how life cycles itself, even as the ocean has high tides and low ones? God made a natural way to keep beaches from being corrupted by letting them be washed regularly. Even so, your little flock will want to have a cycle in its activities.

From time to time, break into the cycle and have a long meeting (four hours) which will include an *Agape* Meal, the "Love Feast" which was used by the early church. It should have the joyful spirit of a family gathering for their Christmas dinner, with some in the kitchen getting things ready, others playing with the children. When all are seated (perhaps at two tables), the meal begins with the first element of the Lord's Supper. Praise songs will be followed by the reading of scripture telling of His crucifixion. There is the passing of a common loaf which has first been broken, with each person taking a piece of it. A time of worshipping in prayer follows. Encourage the children to share in the prayer time. Then the meal is served. The usual table talk will have been influenced by the way it began.

At the close of the meal, the scripture is again read and there is a prayer of thanksgiving for the cup. It is passed from person to person, each one drinking in turn. (Those with colds may be given separate cups to use.) There is then a season of praise.

Following this, have a group play time together, go for a mile walk, or whatever will give the adults and children opportunity to truly enjoy each other. After this, you may wish to let the children go off with one of the adults for a special time in the Scriptures, while the group shares together.

Have *Agape* Feasts as often as your flock wishes to have one. The preparation of the meal is extra work, of course, and those preparing will be the ones to consult. An *Agape* Feast preempts the regular gathering of the week whenever it takes place, even if it is held at other than the normal time.

THE CYCLE EXPLAINED

The following diagram shows a typical ten week cycle. The dark portion of each column shows the amount of the 90–minute session which should be devoted to "Ice Breaking,"

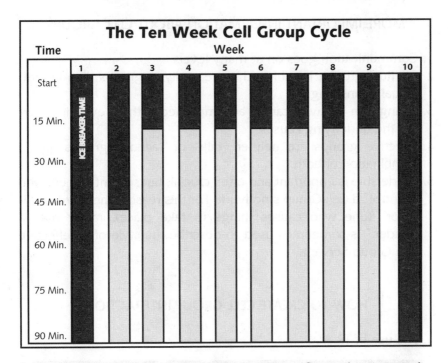

the get-acquainted time. The light portion reflects the time to be used for discussion. Note that the very first meeting is all devoted to getting acquainted. (The Quaker/Friendship Questions are excellent for this purpose.)

The second meeting again requires half the time for this purpose. Sessions three though nine require about ten to fifteen minutes for ice breaking. Session Ten is a sort of "Laugh n' Giggle Party," when the group breaks the pace for some fellowship and playing together. This should not take the form of something like attending a play together, where there will be no interaction. Instead, it might be a round-robin parlor game, or an overnight camping trip, or going out to eat together.

Why devote time to "Ice Breaking?" You will learn through experience that people are like ball teams: they need to "warm up" before they begin to play! If you dig right into the session without any warm up time, you'll have problems. (We'll have more about "Ice Breaking" later on . . .)

MORE IMPORTANT INFORMATION ABOUT CELL GROUPS

1. Communication goes on at many levels.
2. Spiritual growth is achieved more easily in groups than in individual counseling.
3. Changes in behavior can be accomplished without ever discovering the underlying causes.
4. Effective groups are neither "talk" or "action" groups, but a combination of both.
5. Leadership is important and often crucial, but servant leaders who "control" a Cell Group smother it. For this reason, the word "facilitator" (one who causes things to take place), rather than a "leader," is sometimes used to describe the style of an effective Cell Group Servant.

HOW TO CREATE CELL GROUP INTERACTION

1. The use of TRIADS

A "triad" is a group of three persons, the smallest size a group can become and still be a group. By breaking the larger Cell Group down into triads, maximum sharing in minimum time can be accomplished. When the specified time for triad projects has elapsed, each one reports to the group and a general discussion follows. This form is also excellent for occasional use during prayer times as different triads focus on different topics. Use triads any time you want depth sharing to take place.

2. The use of ROLE PLAYING

Assign roles to different members of the Cell Group to illustrate a particular idea, story, or principle.

3. The use of FEEDBACK

Often a Cell Group session will dramatically focus on one, two, or three of the members. They may share special needs or be experiencing special problems. These might become the focal point of the discussion. The Cell Group will work hard to meet these needs or to learn from them. However, needs being faced by others may go unmet because of this limited focus within the session.

When this takes place, you may need to gently interrupt by saying, "We have been relating in a special way to Mary and Jim for

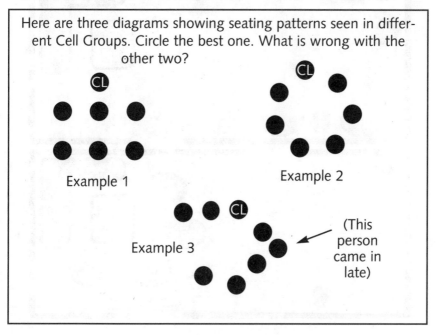

Here are three diagrams showing seating patterns seen in different Cell Groups. Circle the best one. What is wrong with the other two?

Example 1

Example 2

Example 3

(This person came in late)

the past 15 minutes. I am wondering what the rest of you have been feeling? Let's pause and ask each person to share their feelings." In this way, you can draw the Cell Group back together.

PHYSICAL SURROUNDINGS ARE IMPORTANT!

Cell Groups can be demolished by any of these conditions:

1. Too much distance between the Cell Group members when seated, as in the diagram below. Move chairs closer, as shown.
2. People sitting like ducks in a row, unable to see each other.
3. People sitting behind other people, rather than in one circle.
4. A telephone ringing every 10 minutes (Take it off the hook!)
5. A dog or cat that makes the round of the Cell Group.
6. A child that does the same, or who whines for attention.
7. A huge vase of flowers on a table in the center of the room on a table.
8. A super-noisy air conditioning system or a radio blaring.
9. Some folks sitting on the floor, others on chairs (Do it one way!).

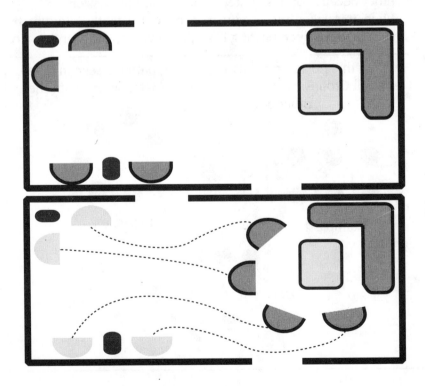

NON-VERBAL SIGNALS

Examples:
1. Boredom, shown by hand on chin.
2. Folded arms, a posture of defensiveness.
3. Hand over face, a statement of shame or embarrassment.
4. A wide smile and words of ice—at the same time!
5. Profuse tears, sweating, flushed face—signs of anxiety.

Learning about how groups work is a process. Always keep a teachable spirit, a keen awareness of people and surroundings and a desire to be a more effective Cell Group Servant.

CELL GROUPS WILL TEACH YOU MORE THAN BOOKS

The best way to learn about the way Cell Groups work is to be in them. There are many good books written about small groups, but groups themselves are your best source of information about them. (You will nod your head and agree with this statement in a few months!)

Communication Patterns in Cell Groups

Here is a formula to explain the number of communication lines in a Cell Group, where:

N=number of people and CL=communication lines:

$$(N \times N) - N = CL$$

Here are some examples:

I talk to you, you talk to me: two CL's.

Another person joins us: now there are six CL's

How many CL's?

_____

NOW, USE THE FORMULA:

With 10 people, how many CL's? _____

With 15 people, how many CL's? _____

Now you know why there cannot be sharing and true community when a Cell Group grows larger than 15.

15

Having Meaningful
Gatherings

Cell Groups become meaningful when they develop true Christian fellowship. This fellowship is the "carrier of the Gospel" to unbelievers in the group. Too often, we preach the Christian message when we ought to be modeling it!

True Christian fellowship is not:

· Studying or praying by yourself.
· Sitting down to have coffee and doughnuts with another Christian.

True Christian fellowship occurs when we allow Christ to open the spiritual dimensions of our lives to one another. The result of being in His light is fellowship with others who are also in His light. He is the basic dynamic of fellowship! If He is missing, fellowship just doesn't happen! And when we set ourselves above those who are unbelievers in the group, we simply drive a wedge between us and them!

But if we walk in the light as He Himself is in the light, we have fellowship with one another and the blood of Jesus His Son cleanses us from all sin. ·*1 John 1:7*

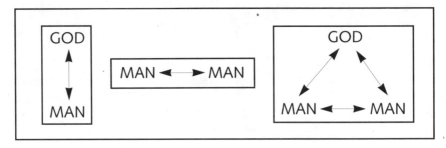

Fellowship is a triangular relationship which exists when at least two believers meet together who already are walking with God. The Christ who indwells them creates a special trust factor within the group. This fellowship becomes a powerful witness of the Gospel. One-on-one evangelism is not able to express this dimension of the Christian lifestyle. It was for this reason Jesus always sent out His disciples in pairs to do His work. Indeed, the only times we find single Christians going to minister was when deep conviction had already occurred, as in the cases of Philip and the Eunuch and Peter and Cornelius.

KEYS FOR BUILDING SUCCESSFUL CHRISTIAN FELLOWSHIP

1. Application and Submission to God's Word
Christ said that if we continue in His Word, we are truly God's disciples (John 8:31). Fellowship means "holding things in common." The basis for those common values, thoughts, actions and attitudes is the Word of God. It is through the application of God's Word to our lives and the submission to God's Word as our absolute authority that we can become what God desires (2 Peter 1:4).

If fellowship within your Cell Group seems shallow and the conversation superficial, then probably God's Word is not central. For the Cell Group to experience meaningful fellowship, the members must filter their lives through the grid of God's Word. Applying God's Word deepens fellowship and turns on spiritual light (Psalm 119:105).

As Christians, we often meet to study the scriptures. In the Cell Group, we will not be doing that. Instead, we will finally take advantage of all those years of study, and we will meet to live the scriptures. We will quote verses from memory more often than we will pick up a Bible and read from it. But the written word will, nevertheless, be central. Jesus said,

If you abide in My Word, then you are truly disciples of Mine; and you shall know the truth and the truth shall make you free. •John 8:31-32

Our application and mutual submission to God's Word establishes the basis for a meaningful Cell Group and true Christian fellowship.

2. Unconditional Acceptance for Each Member

In John 17:21-23, Jesus prayed that we would all be one in Him. There is no room for favoritism and biased attitudes. Unconditional acceptance unlooses the spiritual dynamics for two or more to become one in Christ.

We must make an unconditional commitment to accept each other where we are. We must then discover how to get along and develop our love. Jesus commands us to "love one another, as I have loved you" (John 13:34). Does Jesus break fellowship with us when we disappoint Him? When we fail him? When we sin against him? Or does he continue to love us, work with us and draw us to himself by that love? He is not pleased with the sin in our lives, but he does not reject us because of it.

Our unconditional acceptance of one another is "loving as Christ loved us." This acceptance does not mean we ignore or condone sin. It does mean we love others in spite of that sin or offense to us and by our love we draw them closer to us, rather than pushing them away. It is a loving relationship that affirms us and accepts us, that causes us to grow more like Jesus. Isn't that how God works with us?

That means, for the one who sins, there are those who will not reject, judge, or ridicule. The Cell Group will help, accept and encourage the journey to Christ-likeness. For the one who is sinned against, it means having to draw upon the supernatural life of Christ within, in order to respond as Christ would respond (Galatians 2:20).

3. Absolute Forgiveness for Each Member

This is a commitment from the Cell Group members to stick and grow where God has planted them. It won't take long for each member to discover that the "living stones" nearby have an "abrasive" effect. One could be irritated and sometimes wrongfully hurt. Why will the members stick together?

*And be kind to one another, tenderhearted, forgiving each other,
just as God in Christ also has forgiven you.* •Ephesians 4:32

For the Apostle Peter, the matter of forgiveness raised a question. He asked the Lord, "How many times shall I forgive my brother when he sins against me? Up to seven times?" (Matthew 18:21) Jesus' answer changed Peter's perspective: "I tell you, not seven times, but seventy times seven" (v.22).

*Blessed are the peacemakers, for they shall be called the
children of God"* •Matthew 5:9

4. Genuine Support and Total Confidentiality

A meaningful Cell Group will provide stability and support for each member. This requires honest sharing and the assurance of complete confidentiality. Anything shared within the Cell Group must be considered privileged. Every Cell Group member must guard what is shared in such a manner.

Stress-filled persons walking life's tightrope need others to hold the life net and give them security. To see that happen for your life, you must be willing to hold the net for someone else. The challenge of Cell Group members is not only walking their own tightrope, but also holding the net for others. The Bible puts it this way:

Bear one another's burdens and thus fulfill the law of Christ.
                                        •Galatians 6:2

This is not easy to do in a society that teaches us "to look out for Number One! Just take care of me and mine!" God specifically teaches us to look out for the needs of others (Philippians 2:3-4).

If this kind of caring and support is to take place, we must first be willing to share our hurts, problems and needs with each other. Then we can respond with the genuine love and support that lends encouragement and growth. This means that we cannot be passive listeners. Rather, we must be an active spiritual participant, entering into that situation and prayerfully getting under the burden.

Love means meeting needs and bearing burdens. As we empathize with the one in need, we must keep one hand on the solid ground of the Word of God, while with the other hand we reach out and pull the person to the safety of God's truth. We can't help if we don't get close enough to touch, but we also can't help if we lose our solid grip on God's Word. Jesus teaches that the Word of God is the solid rock upon which to build our lives (Matthew 7:24-25).

HIDDEN AGENDAS IN CELL GROUPS

THE FORMAL AGENDA
CELL GROUP NEEDS
PERSONAL NEEDS

As a Shepherd, you are in a special position to know the needs of the members of your Cell Group. Along with this opportunity comes responsibility.

As your Cell Group meets from month to month, there will be two "hidden agendas" present. It will take a little time for you to be able to fully sense their presence. As you become more experienced, you will recognize them unconsciously and react accordingly to them.

Level One: THE FORMAL AGENDA
(Stated Agenda)

Level Two: Cell Group NEEDS
(Hidden Agenda)

Level Three: PERSONAL NEEDS
(Hidden Agenda)

EXAMPLE: You may be discussing, "Why do good things happen to bad people and bad things happen to good people?" That is the stated agenda for the Cell Group meeting. The topic may touch two hidden agendas:

1. Personal Needs

The first will be the many unspoken PERSONAL NEEDS within the Cell Group. Unknown to you, perhaps the Cell Group includes a person who has been involved in secret sin. This person feels guilty, unworthy, a "bad person." Irritation or hostility may accompany comments made by this person during the discussion time. These special reactions should signal you to spend some personal time with this individual. Your sensitivity will draw out the "true agenda" and will lead you to provide a critical ministry to this life.

Another person responds in a different way: the HIDDEN AGENDA in this life is the result of watching a godly mother die painfully from an incurable disease. Bad things happening to good people? Why should it happen? Why should this mother be subjected to such an end, after living a selfless life? Your ministry to this person is totally different.

2. Cell Group Needs

As the Cell Group meets together, special needs will develop. If one person dominates the discussions, the Cell Group may feel anger toward the offender. This "HIDDEN AGENDA" is a signal to you. The issue of the dominator must be dealt with by you, the Cell Group Leader, or the Cell Group will eventually deal with it! Sometimes groups can be pretty tough on such a person. It is better to be sensitive to the needs of the Cell Group and to deal with such issues privately.

In case of a dominator, the best way to handle this is on a one-to-one basis. The person may not be aware of how much the Cell Group is being controlled and will really try to adjust. Lovingly confronting such a person may not be the normal way you handle problems, and if this is the case you may need to ask your Zone Supervisor to help.

Other hidden agendas which the Cell Group may face can include several members facing similar crises at the same time: unemployment, sickness, tragedy, etc. In these special times, the entire Cell Group can minister to those who have special needs.

EDIFICATION IS OUR GOAL

Moving the Cell Group into the deepest levels of the Spirit brings an entirely new dimension to the gatherings. We have already spoken of the "*oikos*," meaning "household." Interestingly enough, the word is used to refer to what we are calling a Cell Group:

> *Consequently, you are no longer foreigners and aliens, but fellow citizens with God's people and members of God's household . . . •Ephesians 2:19*

> *. . . you will know how people ought to conduct themselves in God's household, which is the church of the living God, the pillar and foundation of the truth. •1 Timothy 3:15*

When the church is called *oikos*, it is quite obvious both by the use of the word and all the scriptures which relate to the activities which transpire around it that it is a reference to the Cell Group of the local church, and not a larger congregation or gathering.

There are two other words attached to the *oikos* family. The first is "*oikonomos*." This word describes a household slave who is entrusted with the wealth of his master, distributing it to the family by giving proper rations at the proper time. We are all members of "The Order of the *Oikonomos*." Thus, the *Oikonomos* refers to a believer who distributes the assets of the Master to those who are in the Cell Group, "God's household."

We must realize the "wealth" which has been entrusted to us is not physical. It's spiritual! And, each one of us has been given a different resource to distribute to God's household, as Paul carefully outlines:

> *Now to each one the manifestation of the Spirit is given for the common good. To one there is given through the Spirit the message of wisdom, to another the message of knowledge by means of the same Spirit, to another faith by the same Spirit, to another gifts of healing by that one Spirit, to another miraculous powers, to another prophecy, to another distinguishing between spirits, to another speaking in different kinds of tongues and to still another the interpretation of tongues. All these are the work of one and the same Spirit and he gives them to each one, just as he determines. The body is a unit, though it is made up of many parts; and though all its parts are many, they form one body. So it is with Christ. For we were all baptized by one Spirit into one*

body—whether Jews or Greeks, slave or free—and we were all given the one Spirit to drink. Now the body is not made up of one part but of many. If the foot should say, "Because I am not a hand, I do not belong to the body," it would not for that reason cease to be part of the body. And if the ear should say, "Because I am not an eye, I do not belong to the body," it would not for that reason cease to be part of the body . . . Now you are the body of Christ and each one of you is a part of it. •1 Corinthians 12:7-16, 27

Paul sees spiritual gifts distributed among us for the common good. Since I need your gift and you need mine, we have a sort of a Divine Cooperative operating, where we give and share equally with one another. (When you meditate on this, it is the obvious result of our being made one Body!)

Let us therefore make every effort to do what leads to peace and to mutual edification. •Romans 14:19

But everyone who prophesies speaks to men for their strengthening, encouragement and comfort. He who speaks in a tongue edifies himself, but he who prophesies edifies the church . . . So it is with you. Since you are eager to have spiritual gifts, try to excel in gifts that build up the church.
•1 Corinthians 14:3, 4, 12

Clearly, it is only in the Cell Group setting, where intimacy and close communion is made possible, that true edification can take place. Thus, in the Cell Group, the goal of the group will be to become true *Oikonomos* Servants of one another, using spiritual gifts to edify one another. It is a *lifestyle*, not something you turn on once a week.

The final word is *oikodomeo*. A word search for the term "edification" and "build up," both commonly used translations, reveals some interesting twists to well-known verses. For example, In 1 Corinthians 3:10, Paul has his ministry as a church planter in mind when he writes, "*By the grace God has given me, I laid a foundation as an expert builder and someone else is building on it.*" He continues, "*But each one should be careful how he builds.*" Here the word *oikodomeo* is used over and over—and it is referring to those who lay the foundation (oikodomeo) of a new church on the foundation of Jesus Christ and builds (*oikodomeo*) on it. He continues (vs. 10-13):

> If any man builds on this foundation using gold, silver, costly stones, wood, hay or straw, his work will be shown for what it is, because the Day will bring it to light. It will be revealed with fire and the fire will test the quality of each man's work.

As you read this verse in the context of what the church was doing in Paul's day, it suddenly has a new impact. You and I are the builders. The gifts are the tools God gives us to use as we build up one another.

> What then shall we say, brothers? When you come together, everyone has a hymn, or a word of instruction, a revelation, a tongue or an interpretation. All of these must be done for the strengthening of the church. •1 Corinthians 14:26

Did you miss that word "*everyone?*" Don't! The church (whether evangelical, charismatic, or pentecostal) has been missing it for as long as I have been alive. The clear teaching of Scripture is that the highest form of spiritual life we can experience is going to take place in a Cell Group, where every single Christian becomes a channel of *charismata* (grace gifts) and the group is built up as a result.

Shepherd, it is possible that you have never experienced what the Bible is talking about here. The first times it happened to me in a group, I knew that the power and presence of God was flowing— but I didn't have enough teaching to realize what was going on.

Furthermore, the blessing of each member flowing with the gifts of God and edifying the Body has powerful evangelistic results. Paul's description of it in 1 Corinthians 14:24-25 points out that a special witness is given to the unbelievers:

> But if an unbeliever or someone who does not understand [Or, some inquirer] comes in while everybody is prophesying, he will be convinced by all that he is a sinner and will be judged by all and the secrets of his heart will be laid bare. So he will fall down and worship God, exclaiming, "God is really among you!"

Can you envision what such a gathering would be like? I can. Let me tell you about one of them:

The praise time was powerful. Every person in the flock who knew the Lord was singing of their love for the Bridegroom. In fact, so dear did His presence become that we just stood and adored him. Some sang softly, others prayed. We were united in our separate adorations.

After we were seated and introductions had been made through the use of an ice breaker, the Shepherd asked if the Lord had given any person a special gift or word for the Body. One dear single parent, with her seven-year-old seated beside her on the floor, said, "Oh, yes! Several days ago He gave me something for the group." She reached over and pushed the "Play" button on a small tape recorder. It began to play orchestrated background music. She sang, "Surely the presence of the Lord is in this place . . ." I found myself choking back tears of joy.

A young father then spoke to us. "This week, as I was reading in Exodus, a word for Robert came from Exodus 33:11. It says, '*The Lord would speak to Moses face to face, as a man speaks with his friend.*' Robert, you have shared with us that all your life you have struggled over God not becoming the real, personal presence for you that you long for Him to be. I have prayed much about that and somehow this verse seems to be for you."

All eyes turned toward Robert. He said, "Let me tell you what has happened! I decided to skip lunches this week and spend the time just talking to God, whether He seemed to be with me or not. I know He is my Father and somehow I felt the block between us was something to be ended. So, every day this week I went to the unused Board Room in our office and prayed. It's the first time in my life I prayed for a full hour at a time. I used portions from the Psalms to praise Him and meditate on Him. This past Thursday, I met Him in a new way! His presence was so real, I could hardly breathe. Thanks for giving me that promise. This has been a very special week for me."

We laid hands on an ailing child and prayed for his healing according to the plan of the Master. We listened to a secretary who told of the stress she faced because her new superior was fearful of his own position and was taking her fears out on her. Wise counsel was given by several in the flock who had endured similar experiences. One told how prayer alone had caused a new relationship to be established with a man who was a tyrant in the office.

In our midst was a dear man, about fifty-five, whose wife had walked out on him. He had come to the group because of the care and concern of one of the flock members. Bless his heart, he didn't know how to dress! The rest of us had on sport shirts, but he came in a black suit and wearing a tie as though he were going to attend a Sunday morning church service.

In the context of our transparency with each other, he poured out his own loneliness and emptiness to us. He had dearly loved his wife and had worked for years to keep her happy. Her loss was worse than her death, for she still lived—rejecting him completely. Oh! How earnest were the prayers for him!

After our intercessory prayer for him, he wept out, "I have never known this kind of love shown to people by strangers. I knew something would happen to me tonight, but I had no idea I would meet God in such a powerful way. I want to give Him my life, but I don't know how. Would someone here show me the way?"

For you can all prophesy in turn so that everyone may be instructed and encouraged. •1 Corinthians 14:31

Don't settle for gatherings where you have a polite time, a nice Bible study, or warm fuzzies in your emotions. Go to your Lord, bring forth the gift He has given you for the Body and let it flow to edify others. Receive from the members of the Body the grace gift which will build you up in your journey toward completeness in Christ.

Oikos, Oikonomos, Oikodomeo—those three words can change your mind forever about Cell Group agendas! When the Head begins to operate in the Body, throw away your notes and go with the flow!

16

Leading the Flock to Experience God

The purpose of your Cell meeting, simply put, is to guide your Group to experience Christ among them. He promises us, "Where two or three come together in my name, there I am with them" (Matthew 18:20). As the presence of Jesus is made real in your midst, people will receive from him encouragement, hope, refreshment and healing.

If you have read the Gospels, I am sure you have noticed that wherever Jesus went his presence drew people like a magnet as people sensed his compassion, power and acceptance. The same is true today. As we allow Christ to be present in our midst, people will inevitably be drawn to Him.

What makes the life of a Cell Group successful is not the presence of a gifted Cell Leader or guitar player, but the presence of Christ among us. As you prepare for Cell gatherings, invite the Holy Spirit to reveal the reality of Christ. That is the specialty of the Spirit of God (John 15:26).

As your Cell Group gathers it is important for people be involved both socially and spiritually. Here is a suggested format:

- Begin with food
- Sit in a circle

- Introductions
- Use an "Ice Breaker"
    - Introduce it
    - Launch it yourself
    - Go in rotation around the circle
- Share a praise time
- Present the discussion topic
- Facilitate the discussion
- Include a "Share the Vision" Emphasis
- Close in group prayer

A helpful and concise way to remember the basic format and purpose of the Cell meetings is with four W's.

Section	Activity	Flow
WELCOME	Ice breaker	You to Me
WORSHIP	Singing	Us to God
WORD	Edification	God to Us
WORKS	Share the Vision	God through Us

Let's look at each of these areas more closely.

WELCOME

A Cell Group must be recreated each time it meets. "Ice breakers"—simple sharing questions or activities—are a great way to help people get in touch with each other and buy into the meeting. They open the way for deeper involvement and sharing in the time that follows. Some principles to remember about ice breakers are:

1. An Ice Breaker must be appropriate for the Cell Group. If it is too childish, people will not feel comfortable. If it is too threatening, people will draw back. Timing is important, also. There are a few Ice Breakers which are best used when the Cell Group is just

forming. There are others which must be delayed until the relationships of the group have been formed.

2. Some Ice Breakers can be used many times. Example: "What was the most important thing that happened this past week?"

3. Always go around the circle, making it plain that everyone is expected to share. Otherwise, shy persons will avoid talking.

4. One problem with Ice Breakers is that they can take up the whole session. Stop this from happening by answering the Ice Breaker first yourself and by not talking more than one or two sentences. Before going on, you might say, "If each one of us takes no more than 30 seconds for our answer, we will be able to share." If someone does talk too long, deliberately look at your watch.

5. Be alert for a person in crisis as the Ice Breaker is shared. It is not unusual for someone to signal they have a real hurt or problem during the Ice Breaker: "I heard this week that my mother has cancer." Obviously, you must return to minister to this need . . . but do not stop the circle of sharing. Say, "We've got to come back to you and share more about that, Susan. Thanks for telling us." Then, continue. This gives Susan a chance to form her comments, which may otherwise just "spill out" more than she feels comfortable sharing with the Cell Group.

WORSHIP

The purpose of this part of the meeting is to connect us to God in worship. Besides singing this may include prayer or Scripture reading. The important thing is that you recognize and welcome the presence of Christ among you. Although this part of a Cell Group meeting is usually simple and short, it is extremely important. If you are not looking to Christ, sharing and ministry in the group will be very limited. How can you make worship as meaningful as possible?

1. Pick singable familiar songs. It is easier to focus on God when you don't have to concentrate on the words and rhythm.

2. Create a typed song sheet for those who may not know the songs by memory. This is very important if you don't want visitors to feel left out.

3. Don't use the time between songs to preach or talk. Let there be more of a flow so that the focus can turn increasingly toward Christ.

WORD

The focus of this time is edification as discussed in the last chapter. In a Cell meeting you aren't trying to convey volumes of new Bible knowledge. The goal is to discover and apply the simple truths of scripture as people in your group reflect on their own experience. Your role as Cell leader is to choose a topic and facilitate a discussion that will open minds and hearts to the voice and power of Christ. How do you choose an appropriate topic? Here are four guidelines:

1. Here's a scripture to guide you:

   Let us consider how to stir up one another to love and good works, not neglecting to meet together . . . but encouraging one another. . . •Hebrews 10:24-25

Each topic should . . .
. . . "stir up" . . . (draw out what is deep within);
. . . "one another" . . . (Mutual sharing, not dominated by one person);
. . . "to love" . . . (Positive, not negative, results; makes people care more, not less);
. . . "and good works" . . . (not "me-centered"; leads each person to have concern for others);
. . . "encourage one another" . . . (At the end, a feeling of having been affirmed, lifted).

2. Characteristics of a Good Topic
• One that will relate to things going on within your Cell Group;
• One that will encourage, stimulate, or challenge;
• One that will confront "fuzzy thinking" about values;

• One that you have discovered by asking the group what topics they feel a need to discuss;
• One that has become a "fire in your bones," that you are "on top of," that has worked itself into reality in your own life and life-style.

3. A Good Topic Meets Felt Needs

The Cell Group is the place where spiritual and emotional support is provided to each member. It is the place where each person's contribution is personal involvement, not knowledge or information. For this to happen, there must be an atmosphere of appreciation, acceptance and support.

4. A Good Topic Draws On Life, Not Knowledge

To understand this, consider the three domains of learning:

Cognitive—This is the area of knowledge. It requires a teacher who can effectively present material. Cognitive subjects are not very appropriate for a Cell Group.

Affective—This area contains our values. It requires a facilitator who can effectively draw out the experiences of those in a Cell Group. Your Cell Group is designed for this category: sharing, not learning. Discussion topics should draw from the experiences of the Cell Group members, not from their knowledge. As a Cell Group Servant, you must be a facilitator, not a teacher.

Psychomotor—This area contains our skills. It involves practice and repetition, in order to perform a skill effectively. Examples of this would be basketball shooting, riding a bike, flying an airplane,

COGNITIVE	AFFECTIVE	PSYCHOMOTOR
Requires a Teacher	Uses a Facilitator	Requires a Coach
Communication is in a "fan shape"	Communication is in a "circle"	Communication is by demonstration
Logic	No Logic	Repetition
Deals with Knowledge	Deals with Values	Deals with Skills

or learning to use a computer. Sometimes a Cell Group may find itself involved in a psychomotor activity, such as the members learning to play guitars. But in such instances, there is little place for spiritual interchange. For this reason, psychomotor activities are discouraged as the focus for a Cell Group.

Your role as a Cell leader is to be a facilitator not a teacher. A teacher is someone who conveys knowledge. A facilitator, on the other hand, guides a group in discovering and applying insights on their own. Notice these contrasts:

There are four parts to effective facilitating. Read over this section until you can recite these four parts from memory. Then seek to implement them in your Cell Group meetings.

1. Provide an Experience.

In the place of a lecture or a teaching, let the group discover something by experiencing it. This is the purpose of small group life! The best way to teach is by putting people in a room with all the chairs facing in the same direction. Teaching is a cognitive process. When you are meeting as a group, the emphasis should be on relational activity, not all sitting in a circle while someone lectures.

Experiences can take on so many hundreds of shapes that it's impossible to list them all. In Part Four (page 191-217), examples will be provided for you to use. As you read over them, you will develop an awareness of what good experiences will do for your group.

2. Get Feedback From the Group

Ask the group, "What did you gain from this experience?" Or, "What new insights do we have?" Or, "What conclusions have we come to?" Get the group to focus together on the results of their activity.

3. Summarize the Group's Conclusions

This is actually for your benefit. Have your own biases colored what you think the group has said in the feedback? Tell them what you think you heard them say and correct any wrong conclusions at once. If you do this regularly, you will know what experience is now appropriate.

COMPARISON: TEACHING AND FACILITATING	
TEACHING	FACILITATING
Provides Information	Provides an Experience
"Fan" Communication, back and forth between teacher and students	"Circle" Communication, often only observed by the Facilitator
Points out logical conclusions	Conclusions are discovered
Written or oral testing of memorized information	Feedback - observed change in values of the disciples

4. Probe for Principles Retained by Group Members

Take a moment to poll every single participant, asking, "What will you carry away from this experience?" This mutual sharing can sometimes trigger a long and heartfelt discussion! I have seen some of the most significant breakthroughs follow this time of sharing.

Our Lord was the all-time best facilitator. He modeled His values as the disciples watched. He shared information in bits and pieces. He kept them in life situations, not in classrooms. He sent them out to try their skills. He allowed them to make mistakes. He let them learn from their peers. He was patient when their values were wrong. He waited for "teachable moments" to occur. He used time as a shaping factor. He used outside circumstances to impart truth. Facilitating was not just a planned activity, but a lifestyle.

Because you are a facilitator, like our Lord, and not a teacher, you won't use in-depth study questions like: "How would people in the first century have understood what Jesus was saying?" Instead, your questions will typically be more simple and direct. Questions like:

• What stands out to you in this passage?
• What is the main point?
• Can you illustrate this truth from an example in your own life?
• In what area of your life do you struggle the most in applying this truth?
• What is God saying to you through this Scripture?

• Where do you need God's help right now?
• If you could ask God for anything right now what would it be?

If you create and choose your questions carefully and prayer-fully, you will often find that you can only cover three or four questions. Notice how the last questions in the examples above are more personal. You will want to use questions like that to help your group personalize and apply what God is saying. This edification portion of the meeting often leads into in-depth prayer and ministry to one another. For these times of prayer you will often want to move into smaller groups of three or four, or men and women. In this way more people can pray and be prayed for.

WORKS

Each Cell session should include a time of "sharing the vision." Here groups recall that they are called not only to enjoy the presence of Christ and experience the power of Christ, but also to extend the purpose of Christ.

Sharing the vision can take a lot of forms as you will see in Part Four of this book, but the purpose is always the same—to move from God ministering to us as a group to God ministering through us.

Occasionally, you will have someone share a testimony of what the group has meant to them. Often, you will use this time to pray for unsaved friends and family members. You can use this portion of your meeting to plan Cell parties for reaching out and building relationships with these unbelievers. Sometimes, your Cell will use this time to plan and pray for a Share Group or Interest Group targeting the felt needs of those you are reaching out to.

Many Cell Churches plan "harvest events"—special services, drama events or activities that present the gospel to people in powerful and appealing ways. Although these events are planned by the church leadership and not be the Cells themselves, they are undergirded by the prayer and personal outreach of the Cells. If your church is planning harvest events, at times you will use your "share the vision" time to pray for these events and to ask the Holy Spirit to guide your Cell members as you invite unbelieving friends.

The four W's of Welcome, Worship, Word and Works provide a general framework for your Cell meeting. At times you may alter the order of these parts or the amount of time you spend on each. But your goal will always be the same: to lead the flock to experience God as they receive Christ's presence, power and purpose.

17

Critical Moments in Cell Group Life

Have you had concerns about how to handle difficult people or sticky situations in gatherings of the flock? Three basic response patterns you may use in these moments are given in 1 Thessalonians 5:14. Paul explains that different personalities require different ways of being cared for. He divides them into three categories and presents different means of helping each one:

And we urge you, brethren, admonish the unruly, encourage the fainthearted, help the weak, be patient with all men.

PROBLEM	METHOD	SOLUTION
THE UNRULY	CHALLENGE	Test and time Be tough Admonish, warn
THE FAINTHEARTED	CHEER	Give examples Be tender Encourage
THE WEAK	CARRY	Take by the hand One step at a time Love, guidance

When praying over the hurting people in your flock, identify which category they fit. You will then know what to say and do in group sessions when they are struggling and need your care. With one, you will gently lead. With another, you will challenge. With someone else, you will believe in them when they cannot believe in themselves.

Always remember that every stress time in group life has a divine purpose. I have met some Shepherds who so feared encounters that their groups grew stale. The athletes have a motto to indicate when the workout has been effective: "No pain, no gain!" That's also true in the flock. Times when hurts are surfaced, when broken hearts overflow, when hidden rage is finally exposed to the Spirit's searchlight, are powerful times.

Ponder the meaning of this verse, which helps us understand some of the dynamics which take place in the critical moments of group life:

> Simon, Simon, behold, Satan has demanded permission to sift you like wheat; but I have prayed for you, that your faith may not fail and you, when once you have turned again, strengthen your brothers." •Luke 22:31-32

Note these details:

> . . . "Satan has demanded permission" . . .

As in Job's case, testing cannot touch us until it has been permitted to pass through the filter of God's protection upon us. Crises within your Cell Group are going to sharpen their spiritual lives. Do not see crises as the result of "luck" or "chance." (Read *Destined for the Throne* and *Don't Waste Your Sorrows* by Paul Billheimer.) But don't neglect YOUR part in the prayer ministry which should enfold the flock during such times!

> . . . "I have prayed for you, that your faith not fail"

Jesus did not seek to stop the painful experience Peter would pass through. Poor Peter had to deal with his egocentric self life before he could be a great servant! But, note the specific kind of praying Jesus did in the circumstance. Jesus saw Peter as he would become, not as he would be in his weakness.

That's important for you to remember as you pray for the Cell Group members by name. See through their weakness, their failure, their sinning and see them as they will become, by God's grace and power. That's what prayer is for . . . the prayer of faith "believes it to be so, when it's not so, because you know God will make it so!"

". . . *and you, when once you have turned again, strengthen your brothers.*"

Note this further prayer of the Shepherd for the sheep; Jesus envisioned the FUTURE MINISTRY of Peter and prayed specifically for it! By faith, He saw past his time of weakness and failure. He saw Peter— strong, victorious and able to bring strength to others. That vision for what God will do in the future should be a mark of your prayer ministry for your Cell Group members and a standard policy for the way you give them help in their gatherings. If God has been willing to believe in us "while we were yet sinners," it is obvious he expects us to have His loving patience with those who are given for us to shepherd.

HOW WOULD YOU DEAL WITH THESE PROBLEMS?

Jeff

You received a telephone call from Jeff the morning after the group had a meeting. He tells you he's going to drop out and is vague about the reason. You remember he talked very little during the group time and slipped out without visiting with anyone when the session was over. What would you do?

Mary Ann

You are in the midst of a group meeting, when you notice that Mary Ann is displaying signs of anxiety: tears, sweating, flushed skin. You are not sure about the cause of her problem. What would you do?

George

It's Saturday afternoon, and you have just settled down to watch a TV movie. You are totally absorbed in the "thriller," and George calls. It seems his father has just had a coronary and is being rushed to the hospital. George is really afraid . . . you can tell by the tremors in his voice he fears for his dad's life. What would you do?

Sarah

Sarah has really been "bugging" you. She talks too much in the group, dominating the conversations. She has a "wise bit of advice" to give everyone about everything. You feel a growing antagonism toward her. You wonder why the group doesn't just put her in her place. What should you do?

Roger

Roger shares in one of the Cell Group gatherings. He informs the flock that the motor on his car has just blown up, and the new job he was to begin in two days has unexpectedly fallen through. He's got enough money to pay the bills for the next couple of weeks, but nothing in reserve to repair the motor. He asks the group for advice. You know Roger is a dependable person who does not sponge off others and has met his responsibilities faithfully for years. He has been faithful to the Lord with the use of his time and his resources. But you also have a girl who you fear might take advantage of anything done for Roger and seek to get financial aid also. In her case, such a gift would only serve to make her more manipulative. What would you do?

Alice

Shattered, she shares the story with the group of a job situation. She has refused to participate in a nasty little scheme some of the other secretaries cooked up to make the boss look bad, hoping to get him fired. She felt she could not go along with them as a Christian . . . but now they have turned on her. Icy stares, critical remarks and caustic insults fill her days. She is trying to decide what to do. How would you lead the group to help her?

Bill and Bertha

This couple have been visiting your Cell Group. You have spent some "one on one" time with them and are just getting to know them well. Neither of them has a strong spiritual foundation and possibly are not even believers as yet. Bertha became verbally abusive to Bill over his inability to make more money. He finally decided he had had enough. He announced to her he was leaving. Weeping, she calls you for help. What would you do?

Donna

This lady is really unstable and unaccountable. She vacillates on fulfilling her obligations and commitments. Now, two hours before the Cell Group is to gather in her home, she calls to say she will have to cancel because she has to use the evening to shop for groceries. What would you do?

18

Get Acquainted Activities

ACTIVITIES FOR USE IN EARLY SESSIONS

These activities may require 45 minutes for 8 persons. They are useful for "kinning" your group members, giving them a sense of belonging to each other. Sometimes it's a good idea to try some of these with your family or a small group of friends or fellow Shepherds before using them with the flock. The main thing to remember is not to ask questions that penetrate too deeply when people don't know each other very well. Keep the activity non-threatening.

In the case of the Friendship Questions presented next, note that all of the details took place "between the ages of seven and twelve." Few people have done things during childhood that would be threatening to discuss with strangers. (That's not true of teenage years, is it?)

FRIENDSHIP QUESTIONS (THE "QUAKER QUESTIONS")

Explain these questions have been used by hundreds of people to get acquainted with each other. None of them require sharing about areas of our life we wish to keep private. Unlike discussion questions, it is best for Friendship Questions to be answered by progressing in order around the circle.

As facilitator, state the first question and then answer it yourself. Your answers will set the tone for all the rest. If you are brief, others will be brief. If you are lengthy in your answers, others will be lengthy. Spend no more than one minute per person on each question:

- Where did you live between the ages of 7 and 12 and how many brothers and sisters did you have?
- What kind of transportation did your family use?
- Who was the person you felt closest to?
- When did God become more than a word to you?

CHIT CHAT (SESSIONS 2-4)

Use any combination of these to break the ice . . .

- What was the happiest moment of your life?
- Tell us about your first date.
- What is the greatest regret of your life?
- The greatest compliment I ever received.
- Let me tell you about my best earthly friend . . .
- The hardest thing I have ever done . . .
- Describe a typical Tuesday in your life.
- My greatest disappointment . . .
- The gift I will never forget (apart from my conversion) . . .
- The thing I most enjoy in my spare time is . . .
- What is your favorite time of day?
- What is one thing you would like your obituary to say about you?
- Share one of your strengths and one of your weaknesses.
- What is your favorite spot in your home or yard?
- My favorite comic strip is . . .
- People might be surprised to find out that I . . .
- Using weather terminology, how would you describe your week—stormy, sunny, partly cloudy, foggy, etc.?

WHAT IF . . . ?

(Can be used in parts over several sessions)

- If you could not fail, what would you like to do?
- If you had to live your life over, what would you change?
- If you were to go to live on the moon and could carry only one thing, what would it be?
- If you could be doing anything you wanted at this time next year, what would it be?
- You have been granted one hour with the leader of our country. What question will you ask? What advice will you offer?
- If you had an all-expenses-paid trip to anywhere in the world, where would you go? Why?
- What would you do if you were to see . . . a person being robbed?
      . . . a person drowning?
      . . . a house on fire?

Get the idea? Now, make up your own!

Part Four

Twelve
Cell Group
Gatherings

19

Cell Group
Sessions

CELL GROUP GUIDELINES

1. Follow the instructions exactly for each session.
2. Insert new material only with permission.
3. Do not use this book when leading a group. Copy the questions on a small card or a slip of paper. The climate will become "class-roomish" if you use your book.
4. Move from home to home. Do not return to the same home two times in a row. Get to know each other on home ground! However, should some not be able to host the group in their home, do not embarrass them.
5. Set meeting dates, times and places four weeks in advance and then schedule one new location at each gathering. Share this information with the group and report it to the central office.
6. Get a map or detailed instructions about how to find each home. Include this in information about the meeting.
7. Always plan three sessions in advance. Always do this planning in conversation with your Intern—never by yourself.
8. Keep refreshments simple. Always serve them as people arrive, never at the end of the meeting. Mingling around the teapot is the first step in group formation.

TELEPHONING AND VISITING

From the very first week, involve all possible members in making phone calls, or in visiting people who have visited the group. It is critical that each person feels needed. The more activities members can do for themselves, the more they will be committed. Sharing "ownership" equally among all group participants will guarantee their further attendance. People who "come and sit" don't last long in Cell Groups!

All this really isn't as much work as it may seem. Most of it will fit into a routine you will soon perform without thinking about it. Like a lot of other things, life is hard by the yard; by the inch, it's a cinch!

SHARE THE VISION: A SPECIAL PART OF EACH CELL GROUP!

In the outlines which follow, there is a section called "SHARE THE VISION." It's an important part of your Cell Group and should never be eliminated. This time period is devoted to telling the story of Cell Group life: what it is, what the dreams for the future are and how newcomers can participate. It is also the time for every Cell member to report the names and needs of unbelievers who are being cultivated.

This activity is part of the Cell Group schedule so participants will keep the vision of reaching the lost. Include on a regular basis the vision of the church as a whole, the vision of the District and the Zone, as well as your own vision for the ministry of the Cell. As Alcoholics Anonymous has constantly expanded because of the commitment of all participants, each one involved in Cell Groups must get the vision of finding others who need to come to Christ.

Scores and scores of persons in our society need a time and place where they can be close to others who will become "family" to them. The traditional church provides many learning experiences such as Sunday School classes, but doesn't possess anything close to the New Testament structure (Acts 2:42-46) for sharing experiences. That's the theme of each "SHARE THE VISION" segment.

LET YOUR INTERN DO THE "SHARE THE VISION"

Give your Intern as much visibility and experience as possible. This brief activity will make all of the participants feel comfortable with him or her becoming the future Servant of part of the group at multiplication time.

Meet together with your Intern after each meeting for an evaluation and planning session. Review the "SHARE THE VISION" reports at that time. The value of this time with each other will quickly become apparent to you!

Cell Group Session One

First, Share the Ground Rules for This Session:

1. We are here for each other. Keep our sharing confidential.
2. The only cause we champion is supporting each other and our sister Cell Groups. Politics and discussion of other organizations we belong to, or meetings to be held elsewhere, are off limits.
3. We will close each session with prayer, acknowledging our dependence on God.
4. Our Cell Group sessions may travel between our homes, opened on a voluntary basis. (This may vary with your culture.)

Ice Breaker (The Main Event):

- Where did you live between the ages of 7 and 12 and how many brothers and sisters did you have?
- What kind of transportation did your family use?
- Who was the person you felt closest to?
- When did God become more than a word to you?

Praise Time (10-15 Minutes)

Use praise songs known to everyone. If necessary, create a typed song sheet for those who may not know the songs by memory. This song sheet is extremely important for those visiting. They may never have heard the songs you are singing. Try to imagine coming into a room full of strangers who know songs you don't know and standing around feeling like an idiot while they all sing!

Presentation of the Sponsor/Sponsee Guidebooks

This may be done in a short time or occupy a good deal of the evening. Helping each person understand its importance will get your group off to a good start. Emphasize that accountability and responsibility are important for us to grow spiritually.

Prayer Time:

Divide the group into triads to pray. Be brief. Mention special needs before breaking up.

Share the Vision (Presentation to be done by Intern)

"Cell Groups are a voluntary act of those who attend them. There is no sponsor, nothing to join, no dues to pay. Our contributions primarily are used to help people who are in need and to cause the spread of the Gospel message. We were formed by the Holy Spirit's activity in people who saw a need and launched the movement. We are a part of (name of church or fellowship). Cell Groups will spread only as we feel they should be made available to bless the lives of others. If you get a lot out of this Cell Group, you may wish to participate in launching a new one at the close of our six to nine months together. We want you to get a vision for helping others as you yourself are helped!

"Before you leave, please pick up a *Journey Guide*. Take it home and reflect on your journey to spiritual maturity and then meet with our Cell Leader and me to reflect with you about insights you gain from it. You can schedule the date and time for that visit right now, if you desire. Some of you will be asked to become Sponsors, and we will talk to privately about that. You will accompany us on these initial visits if we are going to see your Sponsee. We'll spend an hour or two alone with you—either in your home or one of ours—whichever you prefer."

Mingle among the participants after the session. Determine how they have responded to the material. Follow up each person with a phone call within 48 hours.

Notes:

_____

_____

_____

_____

Cell Group Session Two

Ice Breaker:
What was the most important event in your life this past week? Take one minute to fill us in on the details.

Praise Time (10-15 Minutes)
Praising works best in a home setting when the group stands in a circle. A Praise Leader should be appointed, who knows praise songs by heart and can sing on tune. The length of the time devoted should not exceed ten to twelve minutes.

Edification Time: Sharing Our Strengths with Others
Scripture: Philippians 3:10-14

1. Why is it important for us to share our strengths with one another? What happens to a relationship when all we have to share with others are our weaknesses?
2. Three strengths which vary in different persons are:
   Analysis, Communication and Organization.
   Which ones of these are your strengths? Let's help each other here . . . how many ways can we use these strengths for the glory of God?
3. "Networking" is a word used by people who create a group where strengths are shared. How can we help each other? How can we become a "network" for each other?
4. How can we support each other this week?

Prayer Time
Ask each person to pray silently for the person to their right and for any other person in the group they feel has a special need. As you circle the group asking for prayer requests, don't hesitate to respond to requests for physical or emotional healing. Put a chair in the middle of the room, have the person who needs prayer sit in it and gather around him or her. Let fervent prayer by several be included in the session before returning to your seats.

Share the Vision

(Presentation to be done by Intern)

"It's important that we 'be there' for each other between group meetings. Our Cell Group is going to establish a Prayer Chain in this session. This is strictly a voluntary activity. If you choose to sign up, you will be called by the person whose name precedes yours. You will then call the person whose name follows yours. This prayer chain will be used to deal with personal needs of group members. For instance, when you have a special concern or crisis, you may put your prayer request on the chain by calling it in to our Shepherd Servant.

(Circulate the Prayer Chain form.)

"As soon as the Cell Leader and I have visited with each one of you, we will begin to go through *The Arrival Kit* on our own. We'll share insights about it in our Sponsor-Sponsee times, and what touches our lives will be seen in our future edification times. In about three months, we'll be talking about us entering one of two ministries we will launch as our outreach to those who do not know our Lord. The first outreach will involve pairs of us who will establish friendships with people seeking the Lord. We may already know them, or they may be visitors to our public meetings. These visits will be made at the times selected by the teams.

"Second, we will also form a team of three who will begin a Share or Interest Group. This team will conduct a separate group from ours each week and will invite people to it who are really turned off by religion and churches. In about three months, we will see the fruits of our ministries as new people come to join our flock.

"We have effective equipping modules to guide us into our ministries. It's not too soon to be praying about which of these two ministries you will enter. We will be happy to talk with you personally after the group meeting is over about the details."

Notes:

_____

_____

_____

_____

Cell Group Session Three

Ice Breaker:
Who has had the greatest influence on your life since we last gathered?

Praise Time (10-15 Minutes)

Edification Time: Relating to the People in Your Life
Scripture: Ephesians 4:29-32

1. What do you think a "Kick the Cat" syndrome is?
2. Insecurity in our own lives triggers insecurity in the people living and working with us. Which people in your life are most affected by your insecurities? Which people affect you most with theirs?
3. What can we do to help those special people in our life who are facing deep depression?
4. How can we "be there" for each other in our Cell Group, so we don't get into the game of "Kick the Cat?"

Prayer Time:
Suggest that those who feel free to pray aloud share a one sentence prayer for someone else in the circle, or for their own needs, or both. Stress that all people do not feel comfortable praying publicly and for that reason we will not ever "go around the circle" and pray; it will always be a voluntary pattern. Therefore, don't get into a habit of waiting until the person beside you prays before you do.

Let the presence of the Holy Spirit come in power among you as you pray! If appropriate, sing a song of praise in the middle of the prayer time. Make it a time of warfare, of prayer for lost unbelievers, of intercession for those who are in rebellion against Christ.

Are you sensitive to the length of time the gatherings are lasting? If you exceed the 90 minute limit, you may lose some fine folks who can't stay beyond that time frame!

Share the Vision: (Presentation to be done by Intern)
"Our Cell Group is beginning to feel like it's a family! It may be that your first impression of someone else is changing. If you feel

others in the group are meeting a real need in your life, tell them so. And if there is someone in the group who irritates you, it is probably because of unresolved conflicts in your past with people who are similar. We need to be careful that we do not transfer old baggage to new friends. A Cell Group is a place where we have come to grow, not to attack. Part of that growing may be to get together with one or two others between our gatherings to get better acquainted. We'd like to encourage that.

"Visiting with you in your homes and reviewing the *Journey Guide* has meant much to us. We will continue to be available to any of you at any time."

Notes:

_____

_____

_____

_____

Cell Group Session Four

Ice Breaker:

What was the most important event in your life during this past week?

Praise Time: (10-15 MINUTES)

Ask one person to read Psalm 108:1-6; if children are present in your group, ask them to read it in unison together for the adults. Then, if you know it, sing the praise song taken from this passage: "Be exalted, O God, above the heavens and Thy glory above all the earth." Share in a season of praise prayers, using short sentences and enjoying being in His presence.

Edification Time: Believing in Ourselves
Scripture: Luke 10:38-42

1. How many of us gain our feeling of significance from our achievements or our accomplishments? Let's take a poll . . .
2. How many of us feel we are on a "roller coaster" of feeling good and bad about ourselves, depending on our successes or our failures?
3. Is it necessary to think poorly of yourself in order to be truly "humble?"
4. What is the difference between "doing your best" and "being the best?"

Prayer Time:

Ask each person to choose a partner and find a little private spot. It's okay to use the halls, stairways, adjoining rooms, etc. Each couple can take a few minutes to share one on one. Then they are to pray for each other. Those who feel more comfortable praying silently are encouraged to do so. Those who wish to pray aloud can also do so.

Share the Vision (Presentation to be done by Cell Leader)

Begin with a testimony. Choose this person a week in advance with the counsel of your Intern. Let the Intern coach the person to be sure there will be a brief (1-3 minutes maximum!) statement, extremely positive, about what this Cell Group has meant. The Intern should mention again that one of the goals is to create at least one new Cell Group after this one is concluded.

Notes:

_____

_____

_____

_____

Cell Group Session Five

Ice Breaker:

What is the best thing that happened to you this week?

Edification Time: Children and the Kingdom

Scripture: Mark 10:13-16

1. Reduce Chapter 12, "Will the Little Children Suffer?" to a ten minute presentation. Using a large newsprint sheet of paper, create an outline of your comments and hang it on a wall in the room where you are meeting.
2. Have the Intern read all the scriptures as you make the presentation.
3. When you have finished, divide the flock into triads (groups of three) and ask each group to deal with a separate question. Choose the most appropriate ones from this list:
   - What are the most common stumbling blocks Christian parents can put in the way of children?
   - Do you really believe that every child has a guardian angel? Do you believe in angels? Explain your answer.
   - Have you had occasion to see what is called "childlike faith"? What made it so unique?
   - Do you think parents really count the cost of caring spiritually for their children before they choose to have them?
   - What can we do for people who are still furious over the way their parents "jammed religion down their throats" when they were kids?
   - What should be our relationship to children in our Cell Group?
   - Is there an opportunity for us to get involved in ministering to children who come from unchurched homes? How should we go about it?
   - What are the spiritual needs of teenagers in our area? What can we do about it?

Praise Time (10-15 Minutes)

Are there children in your group? If so, focus on them . . . songs they would like to sing, verses they would like to share. Teach them how to praise in prayer. First discuss the truth with them, then show them how, then encourage them to praise in prayer. Close with several praise songs they will either know or can learn.

Prayer Time:
Suggest that each person choose a different partner than last week and that they share and pray in the same way. Indicate this is a time in the Cell Group activity when we can grow closer to each other by these quiet times together.

Share the Vision (Presentation to be done by Cell Leader)
"Each of our Cell Group experiences are unique. This means that new people can be invited to join us at any time. Those who now begin with us can look forward to the time we have grown large enough to begin mother and daughter Cell Groups to replace ours. Who do you know who would enjoy our group? The person may be an unchurched Christian, or an unbeliever. Would you be willing to bring them next time as your guest? We're going to have a 'guest night.' It will take the form of a two hour session and all of us are asked to bring enough food for ourselves and our guests plus one more person.

"This will be the first of many times when we will deliberately open our group meeting to others. You are asked to avoid hanging around each other and spend your time with our guests. Also, avoid the use of all the religious cliché words Christians often use so tactlessly. Let's mirror genuineness, transparency and a true love for each person."

Notes:

_____

_____

_____

_____

Cell Group Session Six

Meal Time

"Yum!"

Create a lovely buffet with the food that is brought. Perhaps candles? Make it more than "ordinary." Wear name tags to identify newcomers and help them to learn your names. Make a fuss over every guest! Don't sit together in clumps: mix.

Ice Breaker:

Who is the best friend you have at this point in your life?

Praise Time: (10-15 Minutes)

Turn the Praise Leader loose and praise!

Edification Time: Personal Titles and Self Esteem

Scripture (Use at end, not beginning): Mark 9:34-35

Role Playing Event: (10-14 Minutes)

This activity shows how titles influence our lives. Send two of the members out of the room, out of earshot. Tell them in private that one of them is the janitor of a small business firm and the other is the president of the firm. They are to role play these positions when they are called to return to the room. The janitor is to act strongly in favor of moving into a new office building; the president is to oppose him in favor of moving into an old one where rents are cheaper.

While they remain out of hearing distance, inform the rest of the group of the two person's identities—but reverse them! The group will consider the "janitor" to be the "president," and vice versa.

When the two people reenter the room and are seated, explain that the entire group, with the exception of the two special people, are to act out the roles of middle management employees of a small business. A decision must be made about moving to new offices. Two possibilities have surfaced: an office in a brand new building, the other in an older building which will need a lot of cleaning up. The choice involves the immediate expense of repairs in the older building, versus the higher rents in the new building. The group is to make a joint decision about which office to select. (Do not disclose the "switch" you have made in identities.)

Let the group work on the problem for at least ten minutes. Take note of those who are silent and draw them into the conversation. Seek to make all present participants in the discussion.

How to Conclude the Role Playing Event

Reveal the "role switch" in the preceding activity. Break up into triads. Give each one a separate question to discuss. Allow five minutes for their sharing. Then call the group together and debrief each triad.

1. How did we favor the opinions of the "President?"
2. Do we agree that "Your Title Is You?" Why, or why not?
3. How many of us have discovered that our significance changed in the eyes of others when we got a promotion with a new title?
4. How closely is the quality of our life related to our personal titles?
5. Why will a "workaholic" be harder hit by the loss of a job than others?
6. Is it sensible to judge the worth of yourself, or others, by the titles or positions held?

Prayer Time:

Break up into groups of three. Pray for each other's personal needs revealed by this activity.

Share the Vision (Presentation to be done by Cell Leader)

Come back together and discuss the following. NOTE: It's time to emphasize bringing new people into the group. The rich flavor of your group is now established and newcomers will immediately feel the love and warmth in it. This will make it easier to "kin" new people and provide the nucleus for the forming of the next group. This is the reason for having the special meal.

The presentation should be very carefully planned in advance. It should briefly summarize what a Cell Group is and what has happened in this particular one to make it meaningful. Arrange in advance for two or three to share (one minute each, please!) what the group has meant to them.

Notes:

_____

_____

Cell Group Session Seven

Ice Breaker:

What was the most significant thing that happened in your life this past week?

Praise Time: (10-15 Minutes)

Assign the planning to the Praise Leader.

Edification Time: Our Work and Our Well Being

Scripture: Psalm 75:6-7

1. Share with us your evaluation of how our work situation affects our general well being.
2. How happy are you on your job?
3. What special problems are you facing related to your work situation?
4. Do job promotions always work out well? Why, or why not?

Prayer Time:

Vary the prayer time by creating "triads"—groups of three—for the prayer sessions tonight. This will take longer than last week. If possible, give an extra 5-8 minutes for the prayer time by shortening the discussion time.

Share the Vision (Presentation to be done by Intern)

After welcoming new members, cover two areas:

1. Discuss the previous session. How did guests respond to it afterwards? What was learned by us which will make our next fellowship night more effective?
2. Go around the group and ask each person to share one or even two accounts of unbelievers they are seeking to share their faith with; focus on strongholds in these lives which need prayer.

Notes:

Cell Group Session Eight

Ice Breaker:
Which Cell Group topic thus far has been most memorable for you?

Praise Time (10-15 Minutes)
Assign the planning to the Praise Leader.

Edification Time: Living With Unresolved Hurts
Scripture: Hebrews 12:15

1. Describe the following situation, without reading from notes:

"A young man was promised the ownership of his father's business if he would give up college and a career as a lawyer he wanted to pursue. He worked hard for his father for eleven years, learning the business at a low level of pay. At this point, his father had a heart attack and died very suddenly. His will ordered the business sold and all funds equally distributed between his wife, four children and seven charities. His own portion was only $15,000. Now in his early thirties, he lives with bitterness over what his father has done to him."

2. How will bitterness within him influence future relationships in his life?
3. What steps could he take to free himself from a prison cell of bitterness?
4. Who do you need to forgive?
5. Who among us has discovered the forgiveness of God in a personal way?
6. Read Ephesians 4:32. Ask, "What does this mean to us?"

Prayer Time:
Ask if there are some who are really struggling with roots of bitterness which need to be dug up and cut out? Spend time with each person in turn, praying as a group for deliverance to be received "right here, right now!" Take authority over these wretched roots that cause such pain and misery.

Share the Vision (Presentation to be done by Intern)

Suggest that some of the new members of the group might like to share their testimonies about why they joined the group and what the conference about their *Journey Guide* has meant to them. As always, talk to those who are going to be asked to share a couple of days in advance so they can be fully prepared.

Notes:

_____

_____

_____

_____

Cell Group Session Nine

Ice Breaker:
What was the most important event in your life this past week?

Praise Time (10-15 Minutes)
Assign the planning to the Praise Leader.

Edification Time: Keeping Commitments
Scripture: Proverbs 27:17

You are not to lead this session! Instead, allow your Intern to do so. Evaluate with him/her the strengths and weaknesses you observed as soon as the session is completed.

1. Why are some people always able to keep commitments they make, like paying a bill on time or being on time for a lunch date, while others are always late?
2. Some have said that people who do not honor their commitments are self-centered. Do you agree with that, or not?
3. Consider two people: one tries to always be on time and the other is always late. Does one feel more guilt than the other if both are thirty-five minutes late for an appointment?
4. How do you feel when someone makes you wait?
5. How do you feel when you make someone else wait?
6. What can we learn about ourselves from this?
7. How can we help one another overcome habits like this one? Is it true that "iron sharpens iron?" Is this something the Lord wants for us?

Prayer Time
Ask the entire group to join hands and pray for one another aloud or silently. Assign one person to launch the prayer and you close when all seem to have had enough time to pray.

Share the Vision (Presentation to be done by Intern)
Indicate that many hours of ministry have already been invested by members of the Cell Group in relating to unreached and unsaved friends. The most valuable contribution this group can make to the salvation of

these friends would be to have a half night of prayer to focus on their strongholds, the spiritual obstacles in their lives that keep them from experiencing Christ. It could begin at 8 p.m. and conclude at midnight, meeting in someone's home. Take 5-10 minutes of the group's time to discuss this. Make plans to hold it on a Friday or a Saturday night.

Notes:

_____

_____

_____

_____

Cell Group Session Ten

A Half Night of Prayer

You may wish to schedule this on a Friday evening. There are many variations on this which will be a great blessing to the flock. Consider the possibilities:

1. Begin with an Agape meal.
   Schedule the evening to begin at 7:00 and continue to midnight. If the children are included, let them share in the first part of the prayer meeting before having a slumber party. (It's even more fun if they can stay all night and sleep on the floor!)

2. Have a presentation on prayer (Use material from the chapter on prayer). This would be appropriate for the Intern to prepare.

3. Break the prayer periods with Praise. (Have the Praise Leader well prepared to lead these sessions.)

4. Vary the evening of prayer between sharing and praying. Let one person at a time share prayer requests and then respond.

5. Set certain periods of time (e.g., 11:00-11:30 p.m.) to pray for specific areas of need. This might include the Share Group contacts and those being reached by the Visitation Team.

6. Occasionally use Triads as prayer groups as the evening progresses.

7. Close by deliberately praying over every person in the room. Move from person to person, laying each life before the Throne as a living sacrifice, holy and acceptable in His sight.

Do you see the possibilities? My first such half nights of prayer are indelibly impressed in my heart and mind and they happened twenty-four years ago! You will never be quite the same after you have learned the joy and excitement and power which is yours by simply becoming a praying Cell Group. The spiritual bonding which takes place cannot be described—it must be experienced.

Notes:

_____

_____

_____

_____

Cell Group Session Eleven

Ice Breaker:
Select one from the list provided in Chapter Eighteen.

Praise Time: (10-15 Minutes)
Assign the planning to the Praise Leader.

Edification Time: Handling Our Debts
Scripture: 2 Corinthians 9:8-11

1. Why do some persons always live within their means and others seem to always be in debt? Does it depend on their earning power?
2. Is the spending of money or buying things attached to our feelings and moods? If so, how?
3. When a ship has to be made lighter to stay afloat, the least valuable items are thrown overboard first. If your debt load required you to do so, what obligations would you throw overboard first?
4. Those who stay out of debt say they set goals for their lives and prioritize their expenditures to relate only to those goals. Have any of us done this?
5. What do we mean when we say that a Christian should have no "second source of wealth"—that God is sufficient?

Prayer Time
Don't lose the momentum from last week's Half Night of Prayer. Allow a longer than usual period for prayer in this session and from now on. When God's people learn to praise and to pray, schedules get thrown to the winds. (That's one reason why this book includes only twelve sessions to get you going. After that, it's up to the Spirit!)

Share the Vision (Presentation to be done by the Cell Leader)
Discuss a group witnessing project. Suggestions: visit a nearby Student Union of a university and interview students, sharing your faith. Hold a street service in an open mall. Visit a park on a sunny afternoon and witness to the people who are there. Visit all the bars in the area and meet the customers.

Notes:

_____

_____

_____

_____

Cell Group Session Twelve

Ice Breaker:
Select one from the list provided in Chapter Seventeen.

Praise Time (10-15 Minutes)
Assign the planning to the Praise Leader.

Edification Time: What Makes a Friendship Last?
Scripture: Proverbs 18:24

1. One writer has said we usually will not make more than 3 to 5 really close friends in one lifetime. Do you agree with this?
2. What are the things that cause a strong bond of friendship to develop between two people?
3. Will geographical proximity influence the strength of a friendship? Why, or why not?
4. How is Jesus a "friend that sticks closer than a brother?" How does the teaching of Galatians 2:20 impact our lifestyles?

Prayer Time:
Repeat the same pattern as last week.

Share the Vision (Presentation to be done by Intern)
About now, the entire Cell Group will be finishing *The Arrival Kit*. Take some time at the close of this session to review the key points of the study. Focus on Week 11's material, and discuss the next stage in your Cell life—being equipped to reach out to "Type A" unbelievers through learning how to use John 3:16. The *Touching Hearts Guidebook* is the tool to do this. Perhaps your church will be conducting a special training time to launch the Cells into this ministry.

You may now be at the halfway mark as you look toward multiplication into two Cells. How do you feel about the ability of your Intern? It's a good idea to turn the leadership of the Cell Group over to him or her for the last six to eight weeks and simply coach in areas that may be a bit undeveloped. The final months of your Cell Group should focus on training to reach "Type A" and "Type B" unbelievers.

You are encouraged as you complete this equipping manual to read *Where Do We Go From Here?* to gain an even stronger grasp of what God is doing through the Cell Church movement around the world.

As the author of this book, I want to close by telling you that each page has been prepared from my own experiences as a Cell Leader, a Zone Supervisor, and a Senior Pastor. It delights my heart to think that the hours spent in preparing this for you will result in precious lives brought into the Kingdom of God!

If we don't have a chance to meet on this earth, I will be waiting to fellowship with you when we enter the future Kingdom of God. For now, I will close by saying, "The Christ Who dwells in me greets the Christ who dwells in you!"

Notes:

_____

_____

_____

_____

Part Five

Shepherding Tools

20

Journey Guide
Helps

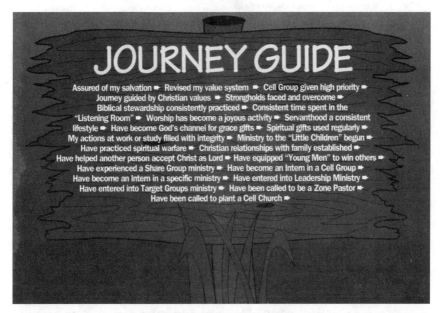

JOURNEY GUIDE

Assured of my salvation ➡ Revised my value system ➡ Cell Group given high priority ➡
Journey guided by Christian values ➡ Strongholds faced and overcome ➡
Biblical stewardship consistently practiced ➡ Consistent time spent in the
"Listening Room" ➡ Worship has become a joyous activity ➡ Servanthood a consistent
lifestyle ➡ Have become God's channel for grace gifts ➡ Spiritual gifts used regularly ➡
My actions at work or study filled with integrity ➡ Ministry to the "Little Children" begun ➡
Have practiced spiritual warfare ➡ Christian relationships with family established ➡
Have helped another person accept Christ as Lord ➡ Have equipped "Young Men" to win others ➡
Have experienced a Share Group ministry ➡ Have become an Intern in a Cell Group ➡
Have become an Intern in a specific ministry ➡ Have entered into Leadership Ministry ➡
Have entered into Target Groups ministry ➡ Have been called to be a Zone Pastor ➡
Have been called to plant a Cell Church ➡

The *Journey Guide* is designed to help you know the spiritual, emotional, and intellectual side of an incoming Cell Group member. As soon as you know a visitor desires to become a member of your group, present them with this booklet.

Ask them to take it home and prayerfully complete each page. Explain there are no right or wrong answers. The purpose of going through the booklet together is for you both to gain insights into the spiritual journey that will take place in the Cell Group.

The *Journey Guide* offers "The Year of Equipping" to each person. It is like the basic training courses that an army gives to its new recruits. Before men are sent into battle, they are trained for what lies ahead for them. Their very lives depend on their training. Spiritually, Christians have many lives depending on being equipped to share their faith. The *Journey Guide* is the planning tool for "The Year of Equipping."

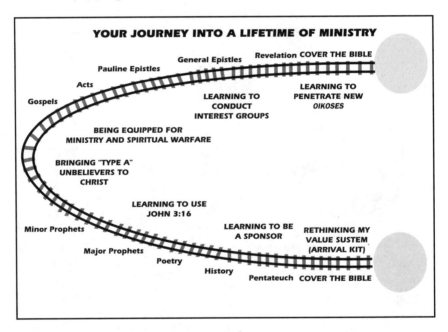

This is the back cover of the *Journey Guide*. It is called a Journey Map. It graphically displays the journey into ministry as a railroad track, and there are "equipping stations" along the way. It takes one year to make this journey.

The first of these two tracks prepares the Christian to know what is between the covers of the Bible. This is done by completing a 1 year course, *Cover the Bible*, which provides five minute cassette taped teaching times. These tapes can be listened to each day, five days a week, for a year. At the end of that time the believer will have a marked Bible and know what each book is about.

The second track equips the Christian for ministry. The first station for a new convert is the *New Believers Station*. This is followed by an eleven week journey through *The Arrival Kit*. This material is written as a workbook, with one pair of pages a day to be completed. It only takes 10-15 minutes for the average person to complete it. It deals with the value system of the believer, comparing the Kingdom values with those we usually have picked up like germs off the street.

The additional modules in this track equip the believer for ministry to "Type A" and "Type B" unbelievers. This entire process should be explained to you in depth as a part of your Cell Leader's Training.

WELCOME TO YOUR SPIRITUAL JOURNEY!

This booklet is like a road map. It will guide you on your journey as you learn to become a servant in the Kingdom of God. You will learn where you are today in your walk with the Lord and what steps you can take to grow into spiritual maturity.

There are no right and wrong answers to these questions. They are designed to help you see what further preparation you need to be an effective minister. Be honest with yourself as you answer these questions. Determining where you need to go requires a clear understanding of where you stand today.

Don't be afraid to evaluate your past Christian growth as you work through the material. Answer each question without worrying about whether it might put you in a "bad light" in someone's eyes. The person reviewing your responses with you will be fully committed to helping you grow in Christ, not to belittling or judging you.

Thoughtfully review each page by yourself. Be sure to use a pen as you evaluate your present spiritual condition. Don't ponder about the way you should respond to the questions! Read and answer them quickly, putting down your first impressions.

After you have finished this guide, your Cell Leader will arrange a meeting with you to discuss insights about yourself—things you discover as you complete the materials. During this private time of sharing, recommendations will be offered to help you develop a fruitful and abundant Christian life.

Together, you and your Cell Leader will create a *Journey Map* for equipping. As you complete that journey a year or so from now, you will be amazed at the growth you will have experienced. Your life will be forever changed as a result of developing your walk with your Lord.

Are you ready? Let us begin . . .

1

When you present this to a Cell Group member, it is good to briefly review this page. It explains that there is no judgment made related to any of the answers.

Your relationship with this person must be based on a spirit of acceptance and not being condemning. Many people grow up in families where they are told their significance depends on their performance. This leaves the person very insecure as an adult.

If you sense the incoming Cell member is anxious about whether you will be impressed or not by the answers, do not try to probe. Just love the person and wait for a deeper trust level to develop between you.

ABOUT YOUR PAST . . .

How long have you been a Christian?

☐ Less than six months.

☐ Less than one year.

☐ Less than two years.

☐ Less than five years.

☐ Other: _____

Your previous exposure to Christianity:

☐ None. I have never read the Bible.

☐ Attended a Christian school.

☐ Previously attended church, but did not believe.

☐ Have never found a church I felt comfortable with.

☐ Have fallen away from following the Lord.

☐ Faithfully participated in the life of a church.

☐ Other: _____

The following members of your family are Christians:

☐ None. I am the first one.

☐ My Mother.

☐ My Father.

☐ Brother(s) or sister(s):_____

☐ Other: _____

Why did you become a Christian?

☐ Influenced by family member(s).

☐ Influenced by friends.

☐ Influenced by respected person (teacher, etc.).

☐ Through preaching or reading Christian literature.

☐ God revealed His presence to me personally.

☐ Other: _____

Have you ever been baptized?_____ When?_____
If so, describe the method (dipped, sprinkled) of baptism:_____

2

What kind of a family does this new Cell Member come from? Has there been a solid faith in the family for a long time, or is this a "first generation" believer from an unbeliever's home?

If this person is able to introduce you to some of the family members on this visit, create a mutual respect between you and each one. In the future, some of these relatives will also come to accept Christ. Who knows? They may be in your Cell Group shortly!

Was your conversion experience:

☐ Dramatic.

☐ Quiet.

☐ Vague.

☐ Often doubted.

☐ Other: _____

Your parents:

☐ Have professed faith in Jesus Christ.

☐ Belong to a church, but seldom attend.

☐ Belong to a church and attend faithfully.

☐ Don't discuss their beliefs with you.

☐ Other: _____

If you are working, how long have you worked?
_____ years _____ months

In that time, how many jobs have you had? _____

What religious groups have you followed in the past?
_____

Write down your past religious or supernatural experiences:
_____
_____
_____

List two or three people who have significantly influenced your life:

1. _____

2. _____

3. _____

How do you share your faith with others?

☐ Naturally, with freedom.

☐ With hesitation.

☐ Rarely.

☐ Out of a guilty compulsion.

☐ Don't know how.

☐ Other: _____

3

Page 3 queries further about the family's religious background. The above page is taken from the edition produced for the United States. A different edition has been released for countries in Asia. One of the differences is in the section, "Do your parents believe in:" In the Asian edition, the list is as follows:

Jesus Christ.
Ancestor Worship.
Buddhism.
No Religion.
Other.

You will want to be sure you secure the version of the *Journey Guide* that best reflects your own culture.

WERE YOU A CHRISTIAN BEFORE ATTENDING OUR CHURCH?

Previous Christian training you have completed:

☐ A New Believer's Course.

☐ A Basic Discipleship Course.

☐ A Course on Spiritual Gifts.

☐ An Evangelism Course.

☐ Other: _____

Previous Christian service you have performed:

☐ Choir/pianist/congregational song leader.

☐ Sunday School teacher/staff.

☐ Elder/Deacon/Department Head.

☐ Youth Worker.

☐ List others below:

_____

_____

What has been your previous attendance in church life?

☐ Sunday Worship: ☐ Regular   ☐ Irregular

☐ Sunday School: ☐ Regular   ☐ Irregular

☐ Prayer Meetings: ☐ Regular   ☐ Irregular

☐ Youth Meetings: ☐ Regular   ☐ Irregular

☐ List or explain others below:

_____

_____

What are the three most unforgettable blessings or lessons you have received from God in your life?

1. _____

2. _____

3. _____

4

Page 4 seeks to get insights into any previous equipping for ministry this person has completed. It also asks about regularity in attending religious services.

The question asking about unforgettable blessings in the past will reflect the depth of fellowship with God this person has already experienced. Does he or she understand what it means to be filled with the Holy Spirit? Usually the answer to this question will give you some indication.

BIBLE KNOWLEDGE QUIZ, PART 1

(For New Believers. If you have been a Christian for 1 year or more, skip to next page.)

Instructions: Write the numbers of items in Column 2
which properly relate to items in Column 1.

_____ The four Gospels

_____ Paul

_____ Emmanuel

_____ Joseph

_____ Peter

_____ Ten Commandments

_____ Turning Water Into Wine

_____ Revelation

_____ Judas

_____ Bethlehem

_____ Twelve

_____ Blood of Jesus

_____ David

_____ Samson

1. First miracle of Jesus.

2. Last book of the Bible.

3. Birthplace of Jesus.

4. Number of Jesus' disciples.

5. Cleanses our sins.

6. Man of great strength.

7. Defeated Goliath.

8. Husband of Mary.

9. Denied Jesus three times.

10. Law given to Moses.

11. Records the life of Jesus.

12. Writer of 13 books of the Bible.

13. Betrayed Jesus.

14. Name of Jesus.

*Check your answers—
See bottom of page 9.*

5

Pages 5 and 6 give two quizzes about Bible knowledge. Page 5 gives a quiz for new believers You will discover there are some who do not have a biblical background at all. Some that you expect to know the Bible do not. Try out the second test on yourself!

BIBLE KNOWLEDGE QUIZ, PART 2

(For those who have been Christians for 1 year or more.)

Instructions: Write the numbers of items in Column 2
which properly relate to items in Column 1.

_____ Gideon

_____ Lot

_____ Paul

_____ Half brother of Jesus

_____ Patmos prisoner

_____ Aaron

_____ Capernaum

_____ Lazarus

_____ Shem, Ham, Japheth

_____ Bethesda

_____ Peter

_____ Elijah

_____ Like a thief

_____ Pentecost

_____ Father of lies

_____ Sword of the Spirit

1. A pool of water.

2. Holy Spirit given.

3. Sons of Noah.

4. Discipled Elisha.

5. A judge of Israel.

6. Cut off a man's ears.

7. Second coming of Jesus.

8. Satan.

9. Word of God.

10. James.

11. Abraham's nephew.

12. Jesus lived there.

13. John.

14. Brother of Moses.

15. Raised from the dead.

16. Discipled Timothy.

*Check your answers—
See bottom of page 9.*

6

HOW WOULD YOU CHARACTERIZE YOUR LIFE?

Write a "T" for true, "M" for most of the time, and "N" for not true:

☐ I look back on my past life with gratefulness and contentment.

☐ If I had my life to live again, I would like to change my past.

☐ I feel life is precious. I am doing my best to live it to the full.

☐ I relate well to other people, including my family and friends.

☐ I have no problem resolving conflicts with others.

☐ I build intimate relationships, receiving and giving love.

☐ I often feel I am not being loved or am unimportant to others.

☐ I am generally transparent, not afraid to let others know me.

☐ I am afraid to let people know intimate things about me. I find it difficult to make close friends and share deeply.

☐ Money has been the most important thing in my life.

☐ In the area of money, I am a contented person. Whether I have much or little, I have learned to be content with what I have.

☐ I find more pleasure in giving than in getting.

☐ After my conversion, I was grounded in my faith.

☐ I have never been discipled by another Christian.

☐ For the past several months, I have been unconcerned about my spiritual life and ministry.

☐ My values are a mixture of those picked up from the world and those which are truly Christian.

☐ I have been committed to Christ's Lordship for some time, and have a desire to fully obey Him.

☐ I have a good understanding about Spiritual Gifts.

☐ I need help in understanding Spiritual Gifts.

☐ I usually reserve time each day to read my Bible and pray.

☐ I am ready to learn about the Bible in depth.

☐ Memorizing scripture is meaningful to me.

☐ I have completely read through the New Testament.

☐ I have completely read through the Old Testament.

☐ I want to learn to share my faith with my friends and family.

☐ I naturally share my faith when it's appropriate.

☐ I have helped another person become a Christian.

☐ I have prayed with several people, helping them accept Christ.

☐ I would like to be involved in bringing totally unchurched people to Jesus Christ.

7

Thoughtfully review the questions asked on this page. Many values are revealed by the answers. Of course, there is a lot of room in these broad questions to falsify inner fears, but you will still gain insights into the value system of this person.

Of course, just visiting in the home will be an enlightening experience for you. You learn a lot about a person's values by observing their surroundings. Do they enjoy excessive luxury? Are they careful with their spending? Is this a matter of economic status, or is it a declaration of values?

Note that this page covers a lot of areas, including personal Bible study habits, the understanding of spiritual gifts, and how they relate to others.

HOW DO YOU LEARN?

☐ I read a lot. Books are important to me when I want to learn.

☐ I seldom read. It's not my lifestyle.

☐ I learn by doing, by watching and being involved in things.

☐ I often listen to cassette tapes. This is a part of my lifestyle.

☐ I like to find someone who knows what I want to know. I will get involved with such a person and develop skills.

☐ I don't have any special pattern for learning. It is not a strength in my life.

Look over the five activities below, ranking them from 1 to 5. Write "1" beside your first preference, "2" beside your second, etc.

_____ Helping other people with their problems.

_____ Going to a party with lots of food and friends.

_____ Working on a computer or making something with my hands.

_____ Playing competitive sports like tennis, etc.

_____ Enjoying music or playing an instrument.

Did your preference not appear above? Write it below:

_____

8

STRONGHOLDS

Scripture talks about "strongholds" in our lives. These are areas where we seem to be constantly facing defeat, discouragement, or fear. We are often unable to move forward in our journey because of them.

Strongholds can defeat us spiritually. They rob us of our peace, love, and deep fellowship with the Father. Heavy periods of stress often enlarge their power.

Are you struggling with areas of life where you feel defeated? Few of us can wrestle with them alone. In the book of Acts, we find frequent examples of people being ministered to by others filled with the Holy Spirit.

Your meetings with your Sponsor or Accountability Partner may be a springboard to victory. Share your strongholds as confidence in him or her develops.

Our Lord Jesus Christ is more powerful than any stronghold, and it is your birthright as God's child to be fully delivered from strongholds in your life.

On the next page, you will find some strongholds common to many people. Prayerfully check each statement that is true for you. Pray as you do so . . .

You will be surprised to discover from the "How Do I Learn?" section that few people these days learn by reading books. For more and more, it's "show and tell time" in the kindergarten of our world. People learn by watching TV, observing others, or taking courses. Many will not learn if you expect them to be a disciplined reader.

This is one of the problems with equipping modules like _The Arrival Kit_. If you have a person in your Cell Group who simply does not read, it doesn't mean they cannot grow in their walk with the Lord. It simply means that instead of a book they need a person to walk beside them and explain the truths.

There is an amazing Cell Church in El Salvador, mentioned in this book, that has grown to 90,000 people in the Cell Groups. When I visited there, I asked to see their training materials. They showed me one sheet of paper! It had all the instructions for their Cell Leaders on one side, and that was all they had ever produced.

As we studied them, we realized that their Cell members were working class people who seldom had time to read. Knowing this, the Zone Pastors verbally taught them. They love the Lord as much or more than the bookworm types!

STRONGHOLDS, Continued

Check the statements which are true or partially true for you. You will be given the opportunity to share in private why you checked the statement.

☐ I had a poor relationship with my father/mother. Perhaps that's why I find it hard to believe that God truly loves me.

☐ I have a hard time forgiving myself for things I've done in the past. I constantly dislike myself.

☐ I have been wrongly treated and hurt in the past. I find it hard to be set free of the inner anger I feel when remembering it.

☐ I have a sin or bad habit in my life that controls me. I try hard, but I really feel like a captive in this situation.

☐ I have a hard time with a sexual problem. I have never been able to break its control and the bad habits that go with it.

☐ I have some addictive behavior: e.g., overeating, gambling, exaggerating, smoking, drugs, alcohol, etc.

☐ I sometimes feel that my desire for money and possessions has a powerful control over me.

☐ Sometimes I find that I cannot control my anger. It seems to well up from within and explodes before I can stop it.

☐ I have a problem with anxiety. Sometimes I don't even know why I am so anxious. I get anxious even about little things.

☐ I have many fears in my life. They include fear of the dark and being alone, fear of sickness and death, etc.

☐ I have contemplated suicide on several occasions.

☐ I have been involved in homosexuality.

☐ I find it hard to concentrate when I am reading the Bible and praying. It is as though a drowsiness comes on me.

☐ In the past, I have been involved in some occult practices (e.g., seances, witchcraft, etc.) or have been a member of a cult.

☐ I have been abused physically, mentally or emotionally.

☐ I still have pornography or sensual books with me in my home.

☐ I have had disappointing experiences with former churches.

☐ I hold up work as my most important activity. My life is consumed by my performance and achievement level.

☐ I find myself sleeping more than normal and have no desire or motivation to do anything productive.

☐ In the past, I have been a zealous idol worshipper.

☐ I still possess idols and charms.

☐ _____.

ANSWERS TO QUIZ ON PAGE 5
1, Turning water into wine; 2, Revelation; 3, Bethlehem; 4, Twelve; 5, Blood of Jesus; 6, Samson; 7, David; 8, Joseph; 9, Peter; 10, Ten Commandments; 11, The Four Gospels; 12, Paul; 13, Judas; 14, Emmanuel
If you scored lower than 11, you really need to take COVER THE BIBLE.

ANSWERS TO QUIZ ON PAGE 6
1, Bethesda; 2, Pentecost; 3, Shem, Ham, Japheth; 4, Elijah; 5, Gideon; 6, Peter; 7, Like a thief; 8, Father of lies; 9, Sword of the Spirit; 10, Half brother of Jesus; 11, Lot; 12, Capernaum; 13, Patmos prisoner; 14, Aaron; 15, Lazarus; 16, Paul
If you scored lower than 11, you really need to take COVER THE BIBLE.

9

Strongholds! How many does this dear Christian live with? How can they be uncovered? The materials on pages 8 and 9 will make the person begin to think about them. However, unless there is a special trust relationship between you, it is too soon to expect any deep confessions. One exception is when the person is hurting so badly that they cannot contain their pain. When this happens, you may need to stay until late at night.

One suggestion, from years of experience with such pain-filled people: if there is a deep confession time in this interview, be sure to call the person soon—within 24 hours—and say, "I want you to know how much your transparency and openness has impressed me. I am certain the Lord has brought us together in the Cell Group so both of us might grow towards Him. May I ask you to begin to pray daily for me? I want you to pray that I will be adequate to minister to you. You are important to me!"

You see, many times after you leave and deep confession has taken place, the person will be feeling, "Oh, dear! Why did I do that? My Cell Leader doesn't know much about me. What is he/she thinking? I am not sure I want to face him/her after all the things we talked about. I am so ashamed!" Just an encouraging word at the right moment will assure the person you are still committed to the relationship.

CELL LIFE IS IMPORTANT TO YOU!

Many people believe that everything we learn must come from reading books or listening to lectures. Many church leaders today receive their primary training this way. Most of what we learn in life is caught, not taught. Most of us learn by observing others and then doing it ourselves. The disciples learned from Jesus this way.

Learning by watching others and imitating them is called modeling. Think of your own life. Have you ever listed the people you have used as a pattern for your own lifestyle? (These may be the same as on page 3.) In the box below, write the names of two people who have filled this special role for you:

1. _____

2. _____

The art of relating to others is not learned from reading books. To learn how to relate, we must watch others relate. Books can give us information about relationships, but we must observe people who are doing what the books talk about!

That is why every person needs parent models along with models of brothers and sisters. These people give us our values. They also set the atmosphere of the greater community. We need relationships with people we can identify with and whose actions we can copy.

The Cell Group is God's most practical design for this modeling to take place among Christians. In the urban world, people often do not understand what it is like to live responsibly with fellow believers. Perhaps your entry into your Cell Group will be the very first time in your life to experience true community.

We learn community by participating in it and not by just observing. Learn to give love as well as receive it. Learn to be sensitive to others. For example, avoid dominating a Cell discussion. This chokes off sharing by other Cell members. Prepare yourself beforehand by listening to God so that you can build up others who need your affirmation.

Enter into the experience with all your heart! There will be more mature Christians you can select as good patterns for your own life. In time, you will become a model to those who are younger than you in Christ.

10

Do not register surprise over anything that is shared. Prayerfully take notice of things that will help you expand your prayer life for this person. Use the special form provided in this manual, preparing one sheet for each person in your Cell. (Read Chapter 7 again.)

Page 10 reviews the meaning of Cell Group life. Buttress it with testimonies about what the Cell has meant to you, to your Intern, and to the Sponsor you have brought along.

There's a really important box on page 10! Be sure you get to know about the two people who have been a pattern for this person's lifestyle. Is it a mother, a father, a best friend, an employer who has taken a special interest in him or her?

It's a good idea to meet these two people if possible. Your time spent with them will give you many insights into how to minister to the new Cell member.

"WOULD YOU BE MY SPONSOR?"

Every Cell Group member should become a part of a living chain of people who love and build up one another. Being helped, and being a helper— this is the pattern of the New Testament church. Perhaps you feel you are a "second class Christian" because you don't know a lot of scripture, or your prayer life is weak. Don't believe this lie. Martin Luther said, "The simplest peasant, armed with the Gospel, is mightier than a Pope!"

Your growth in Christ will depend on your being attached to someone in your Cell Group who has taken three or four steps ahead of you, and who can show you where to put your feet as you journey toward maturity.

One of the ministries of your Cell Leader is to arrange for you to work with another Cell member who can build you up by meeting with you on a regular basis. Seek his or her guidance to discover who should become your Sponsor. Even as you join hands with this person, there will be someone just a few steps behind you who needs you. Thus, as you grow in your faith, you will soon begin to hold the hand of another person who needs your guidance. You'll minister to your Sponsee and also become a guide as a Sponsor. You need not worry about your effectiveness, for your own Sponsor will always be there to help you as you minister to someone else. If your Sponsor doesn't know how to help you, someone in the chain will be available.

Keep in touch with your Sponsor. Meet together weekly. In addition, there will be special needs which may cause you to spend hours together, as good friends do. Although your Cell Leader will always be available to you, your primary helper will be your own Sponsor.

Your Sponsor, you, and your Sponsee create a special "triplet" for prayer and sharing. As your group multiplies, usually every six months or so, you will create new links—but the old ones won't fade away!

11

With the review of this page, allow the Sponsor who has accompanied you to take over for a few minutes. There needs to be a bonding in this interview between these two, and you can help by encouraging conversation. I have even used the Quaker Questions in this circumstance to acquaint the new person with myself, the Intern, and the Sponsor.

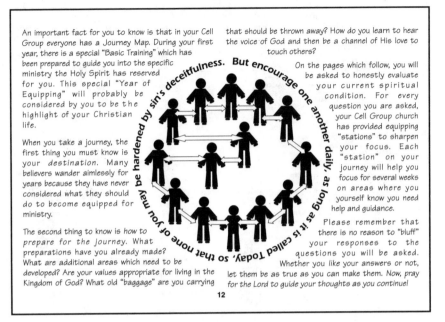

An important fact for you to know is that in your Cell Group everyone has a Journey Map. During your first year, there is a special "Basic Training" which has been prepared to guide you into the specific ministry the Holy Spirit has reserved for you. This special "Year of Equipping" will probably be considered by you to be the highlight of your Christian life.

When you take a journey, the first thing you must know is your *destination*. Many believers wander aimlessly for years because they have never considered what they should do to become equipped for ministry.

The second thing to know is how to prepare for the journey. What preparations have you already made? What are additional areas which need to be developed? Are your *values* appropriate for living in the Kingdom of God? What old "baggage" are you carrying that should be thrown away? How do you learn to hear the voice of God and then be a channel of His love to touch others?

On the pages which follow, you will be asked to honestly evaluate your current spiritual condition. For every question you are asked, your Cell Group church has provided equipping "stations" to sharpen your focus. Each "station" on your journey will help you focus for several weeks on areas where you yourself know you need help and guidance.

Please remember that there is no reason to "bluff" your responses to the questions you will be asked. Whether you *like* your answers or not, let them be as true as you can make them. Now, pray for the Lord to guide your thoughts as you continue!

12

Reviewing pages 13 and 14 will be the climax of the time you spend together. Discuss all that are checked off, and note carefully the ones that are not. Note that wherever deficiencies are admitted, there is a code to suggest equipping modules which can be taken.

JOURNEY GUIDE EVALUATION FORM

(+, True; —, Not Yet)

____ STATION 1: ASSURED OF MY SALVATION
You understand what it means to become a Christian and enter the Kingdom of God and have told this to another person by sharing your experience and the scriptures. (AK, THG)

____ STATION 2: REVISED MY VALUE SYSTEM
You discern personal values which are not appropriate to your journey and are adding others which need to be added to your lifestyle. (CTB, AK)

____ STATION 3: CELL GROUP GIVEN HIGH PRIORITY
You have a strong sense of belonging to God's family and seek to build up your fellow Cell Group members by making your participation the highest priority of your journey. (AK)

____ STATION 4: JOURNEY GUIDED BY CHRISTIAN VALUES
You understand the various journeys in "The Year of Equipping" and have committed yourself to complete them in order to prepare for a lifetime of service and ministry. (CTB, AK)

____ STATION 5: STRONGHOLDS FACED AND OVERCOME
You have identified strongholds in your own life and have received ministry from your Cell Group or Pastoral Team members to experience the breaking down of each one. (AK, CTB)

____ STATION 6: BIBLICAL STEWARDSHIP CONSISTENTLY PRACTICED
You recognize that it is the task of a servant to obey his Master, and that the Master will provide for all your needs. Therefore, you are faithful in tithing and to support the ministry of your Cell Group church. (AK, CTB)

____ STATION 7: CONSISTENT TIME SPENT IN THE "LISTENING ROOM"
You know how to pray and demonstrate your dependence on God through developing a daily time in the "Listening Room." You respond to life circumstances by praying. (AK)

____ STATION 8: WORSHIP HAS BECOME A JOYOUS ACTIVITY
You experience the presence of God through personal and corporate worship. (AK)

____ STATION 9: SERVANTHOOD A CONSISTENT LIFESTYLE
You are sensitive to the needs of others and demonstrate a willingness to serve others even in menial tasks. You are impartial in those you serve. (AK, THG)

____ STATION 10: HAVE BECOME GOD'S CHANNEL FOR GRACE GIFTS
You realize the importance of being filled with the Holy Spirit and have fully submitted yourself to being a channel for His spiritual gifts to flow into ministry. (AK, CTB)

____ STATION 11: SPIRITUAL GIFTS USED REGULARLY
You consistently experience the filling of the Holy Spirit and flow with His gifts to build up fellow believers, participate in ministry times for healing and deliverance, and to evangelize unreached persons. (AK, CTB, SWW)

____ STATION 12: MY ACTIONS AT WORK OR STUDY FILLED WITH INTEGRITY
Your conduct at work or study demonstrates the highest levels of integrity. (AK, CTB)

____ STATION 13: MINISTRY TO "LITTLE CHILDREN" BEGUN
You have become a "Sponsor" for a newborn Christian. You are sensitive to the needs of hurting people in your Cell Group and care and pray for them. (AK, CTB)

13

____ STATION 14: HAVE PRACTICED SPIRITUAL WARFARE
You have learned to confront the power of Satan in the lives of others and in geographical areas, and prevail against it with authority. (AK, CTB, THG)

____ STATION 15: CHRISTIAN RELATIONSHIPS WITH FAMILY ESTABLISHED
You have learned how to live with those in your immediate and extended family in a manner that glorifies God and reveals your life in the Kingdom of God. (AK, CTB, THG)

____ STATION 16: HAVE HELPED ANOTHER PERSON ACCEPT CHRIST AS LORD
You have experienced sharing the gospel with others and have led another person to receive Christ as Lord, and have established him/her as a part of your Cell Group. (THG)

____ STATION 17: HAVE EQUIPPED "YOUNG MEN" TO WIN OTHERS
You have helped another Cell Group member learn to share John 3:16 and have seen him/her bring a lost person to Christ and into the Cell Group. (THG)

____ STATION 18: HAVE EXPERIENCED A SHARE (INTEREST) GROUP
You have participated with two or three other Cell Group members in establishing a Share (Interest) Group for unresponsive persons and have seen a new believer brought into the Cell. (BB, BG, BA)

____ STATION 19: HAVE BECOME AN INTERN IN A CELL GROUP
You have felt called to lead a Cell group and have entered training as an Intern. (AM)

____ STATION 20: HAVE BECOME AN INTERN IN A SPECIFIC MINISTRY
You have accepted God's call to lead a Cell Group and are able to assist the Cell Leader in the ministry, OR you have become equipped to minister in other areas of the Cell church, including music, counselling, evangelism, deliverance, teaching, etc. (AM)

____ STATION 21: HAVE ENTERED INTO LEADERSHIP MINISTRY
You have developed a Shepherd's heart and have become responsible for leading others into ministries. You have led a specific ministry and have equipped an Intern to replace you, at the level of leading a Cell or serving as a Zone Supervisor. (AM)

____ STATION 22: HAVE ENTERED INTO TARGET GROUPS MINISTRY
You have been called by the Lord to reach a special group for the Lord, and are constantly involved in targeting them through involvement in Share (Interest) Groups. (BG, BA)

____ STATION 23: HAVE BEEN CALLED TO BE A ZONE PASTOR
You have rearranged your affairs and have been accepted by your church to be trained as a Zone Pastor Intern, and are prepared to enter The Equipping Stations System for a year of intensive training. (AM)

____ STATION 24: HAVE BEEN CALLED TO PLANT A CELL CHURCH
You have experienced the life of a Zone Pastor and have been affirmed by the Leadership Team as being called to plant new work in your own culture or another part of the world. You have been sent as a part of a Church Planting Team, supported by your sending church. (AM)

THESE ARE THE RECOMMENDED MODULES FOR YOUR JOURNEY INTO MINISTRY

The symbols below are shown at the end of various Stations to help you chart your Journey with your Cell Leader.

MODULES A, B, C, D: COVER THE BIBLE (CTB)
MODULE 1: THE ARRIVAL KIT (AK)
MODULE 2: TOUCHING HEARTS GUIDEBOOK (THG)
MODULE 3: SPIRITUAL WARFARE WEEKEND (SWW)
MODULE 4: BUILDING BRIDGES, OPENING HEARTS (BB)
MODULE 5: BUILDING GROUPS, OPENING HEARTS (BG)
MODULE 6: BUILDING AWARENESS, OPENING HEARTS (BA)
MODULES 7-BEYOND: ADVANCED MODULES (AM)

14

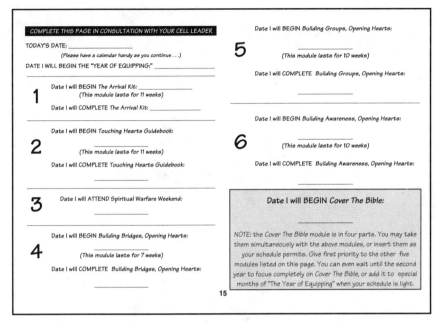

COMPLETE THIS PAGE IN CONSULTATION WITH YOUR CELL LEADER

TODAY'S DATE: _____
        (Please have a calendar handy as you continue . . .)
DATE I WILL BEGIN THE "YEAR OF EQUIPPING:" _____

1 Date I will BEGIN The Arrival Kit: _____
        (This module lasts for 11 weeks)
    Date I will COMPLETE The Arrival Kit: _____

2 Date I will BEGIN Touching Hearts Guidebook:
        _____
        (This module lasts for 11 weeks)
    Date I will COMPLETE Touching Hearts Guidebook:
        _____

3 Date I will ATTEND Spiritual Warfare Weekend:
        _____

4 Date I will BEGIN Building Bridges, Opening Hearts:
        _____
        (This module lasts for 7 weeks)
    Date I will COMPLETE Building Bridges, Opening Hearts:
        _____

Date I will BEGIN Building Groups, Opening Hearts:

5   _____
        (This module lasts for 10 weeks)

    Date I will COMPLETE Building Groups, Opening Hearts:

        _____

    Date I will BEGIN Building Awareness, Opening Hearts:

6   _____
        (This module lasts for 10 weeks)

    Date I will COMPLETE Building Awareness, Opening Hearts:

        _____

Date I will BEGIN Cover The Bible:

NOTE: the Cover The Bible module is in four parts. You may take them simultaneously with the above modules, or insert them as your schedule permits. Give first priority to the other five modules listed on this page. You can even wait until the second year to focus completely on Cover The Bible, or add it to special months of "The Year of Equipping" when your schedule is light.

15

Page 15 actually creates a calendar for The Year of Equipping. It is a good idea to take a calendar with you when you visit. Do not leave this page blank! It is important that this incoming Cell member be prepared for ministry.

Notice there is a special section for you use to encourage *Cover the Bible* to be completed. It is a modern tragedy that most Christians have to go to church on Sunday to hear what the Bible teaches. While not all believers are Bible scholars, all Cell members should be exposed to the Scripture so that they can search it for themselves.

HOW TO PREPARE YOUR PERSONAL TESTIMONY

Thoughtfully recall your conversion experience. Then write no more than two or three sentences describing it, using this outline taken from Paul's testimony in Acts 26:1-28:

MY LIFE BEFORE BECOMING A CHRISTIAN WAS LIKE THIS:

_____
_____
_____
_____
_____
_____

THIS IS THE WAY I REALIZED THAT I NEEDED TO FOLLOW JESUS:

_____
_____
_____
_____
_____
_____

THESE ARE THE DETAILS OF HOW I ACTUALLY ACCEPTED CHRIST:

_____
_____
_____
_____
_____
_____

THIS IS WHAT IT MEANS TO ME TO BE A CHRISTIAN:

_____
_____
_____
_____
_____

. . . CLOSE BY ASKING, "HAS THIS EVER HAPPENED TO YOU?

16

Last, but not certainly least—if this page has been filled out in advance, review it carefully with the new Cell member. Discuss the details of it to get it into your own mind.

Ask, "Is there someone in your life who needs to hear what I just heard? Is there someone you feel you would like to tell about how you became a Christian? If you are fearful to do so, I will be glad to go with you and help you introduce your testimony." Such encouragement from you may cause another person to enter the Kingdom, and you will have set the pace as a spiritual leader.

May God richly bless you as you experience the *Journey Guide* interview for the first time!

21

Useful Forms

The forms which follow are for your use as you feel they will be helpful to you in your ministry. All are optional except the REPORT OF CELL GROUP MEETING. Your Cell Church will probably have a replacement for the one in this book, which is provided as a model.

It is mandatory that a weekly report be sent to the Zone office following every meeting! There should be not a single deviation from the habit of faxing, telephoning, or turning in this report within 24 hours of the time your group meeting. This may be delegated to one of the Cell Group members.

Permission is hereby granted to duplicate these forms for your personal use.

Page 239: CELL GROUP COVENANT
You may feel this has special value in bonding the group members together. Some groups really respond to a written Covenant, others don't. Decide for yourself if it has usefulness in the context of your community.

Page 240: REPORT OF CELL GROUP MEETING
In triplicate. Keep bottom copy. Turn in second copy to the person you are training to be a Cell Group LEADER. Top copy to Cell Group office.

Page 241: JOURNEY GUIDE INTERVIEW
Use this outline every time you meet with a flock member to help them plan further preparation for ministry and service.

Page 242: CELL GROUP FLOCK
Use for a permanent record of names and vital statistics of flock members. In case of death or emergency, get Next of Kin information.

Page 243: CELL GROUP GUEST LIST
Can be copied and sheet passed around in gatherings to get information on guests who are present. (White out page heading and number.)

Page 244: CELL GROUP ATTENDANCE: _____ QUARTER
Room for 21 names. If you have a larger base than that, photocopy the sheets.

Page 245: CELL LEADER'S SELF-EVALUATION FORM

Page 246: INTERN EVALUATION FORM
Use the first form for checking up on yourself. Use the Evaluating Your Intern form to discuss his/her ministry.

Page 247: PRAYER CHAIN
Pass a copy of this around the group for each person to sign. Each person will be called by the person whose name is above theirs. They will call the person whose name is below theirs. If there is no answer, the following name on the list is to be called. Reproduce a copy of this for each member.

Page 248: CELL GROUP MEETING EVALUATION

Page 249: CELL GROUP PLANNING SHEET
Useful for times you spend with your Cell Group Intern Trainee. Preserved, they give you insights into patterns you have observed as the group matures.

Page 250: TOPIC PLANNING SHEET
Useful in planning Edification Times.

A Cell Group Covenant

*Knowing that Christ has brought me His peace,
I will offer it to those who have none.*

*Knowing that an individual Cell Group
session may be the turning point for a life,
I place my participation in this ministry
at the very top of my priority list.*

*I will do my best to bring two or three persons
to my group during each of its cycles.*

*I will help those who are in deep distress,
patiently working with them until they are able
to choose whether they wish to respond to
Christ's unconditional love.
I will respond to all with God's acceptance;
I will not be judgmental.
I will always remember that God allows all things
for His eternal purposes.*

*I will prayerfully seek to know what, in
each situation, God wants to address . . .
and be His voice of compassion.*

*I will earnestly avoid giving simplistic
"solutions" to difficult situations.*

*Signed:*_____

REPORT OF CELL GROUP MEETING

Area   Name of Host

Address where we met   Total Present   Total Visitors

Date of Meeting   Day of Week   Time

Cell Leader   Intern   Praise Leader

LIST OF ALL THOSE ATTENDING
If this is the first time, underline the name!
Write full name, address and telephones on back of sheet.

NAME	NAME

INFORMATION ABOUT NEXT CELL GROUP MEETING

Date of Meeting	Day of Week S M T W TH F S	Time AM PM
Name of Host	Telephone	Address of Next Meeting

IMPORTANT: Return top copy to Cell Group Office Within 24 hours of meeting!

JOURNEY GUIDE INTERVIEW

How long a Christian?

Any lapses in the past?

Previous Christian training?

Previous Christian service?

In past, how active in church life?

Conversion experience: questionable?

Faith Sharing in past?

Bible Knowledge Quiz: Score?

Awareness of Spiritual Gifts?

Gifts actively used? None.

Is there a consistent pattern of prayer?

Is there a consistent pattern of Bible study?

Led anyone to Christ?

How does this person learn?

Did material on Strongholds surface anything?

Any strongholds?

Aware of Cell Group lifestyle? Ready to commit?

Feelings about having, then becoming, a Sponsor?

Readiness for outreach?

After you have completed the interview and are alone, write down your thoughts about this person while they are fresh in your mind. List stress areas you have discerned. Then turn to the FORMS section and create an INTERCESSORY PRAYER LIST for this person.

THOUGHTS:

CELL GROUP FLOCK

Name_____

Address_____

City_____ ST_____ Zip_____

Tel. (H)_____(W)_____

Next of Kin_____Tel._____

Name_____

Address_____

City_____ ST_____ Zip_____

Tel. (H)_____(W)_____

Next of Kin_____Tel._____

Name_____

Address_____

City_____ ST_____ Zip_____

Tel. (H)_____(W)_____

Next of Kin_____Tel._____

Name_____

Address_____

City_____ ST_____ Zip_____

Tel. (H)_____(W)_____

Next of Kin_____Tel._____

Name_____

Address_____

City_____ ST_____ Zip_____

Tel. (H)_____(W)_____

Next of Kin_____Tel._____

GUEST LIST

Name_____

   Address_____

   City_____ST_____Zip_____

   Tel. (H)_____(W)_____

   Remarks:_____

Name_____

   Address_____

   City_____ST_____Zip_____

   Tel. (H)_____(W)_____

   Remarks:_____

Name_____

   Address_____

   City_____ST_____Zip_____

   Tel. (H)_____(W)_____

   Remarks:_____

Name_____

   Address_____

   City_____ST_____Zip_____

   Tel. (H)_____(W)_____

   Remarks:_____

Name_____

   Address_____

   City_____ST_____Zip_____

   Tel. (H)_____(W)_____

   Remarks:_____

CELL GROUP Attendance: _____ Quarter

√ = Present

Member's Name	Week												
	1	2	3	4	5	6	7	8	9	10	11	12	13

CELL LEADER'S SELF-EVALUATION FORM

TASK	LEVEL OF EXCELLENCE (10=HIGH; 1=LOW)									
	10	9	8	7	6	5	4	3	2	1
Has visited every Cell member at home										
Relates well to visitors										
Conscientiously "kins" new members										
Participates in discussions										
Brings unbelievers to Share Group										
Is taking, has taken, Shepherd training										
Coordinates visitation										
Personally makes visits										
Conducts Cell meetings effectively										
Well prepared to facilitate topics										
Effectively presents Share the Vision										
Sensitive to needs during discussions										
Lovingly cares for problemed people										
Leads Prayer Chain activity										
Prays consistently for members										
Keeps efficient records										
Conscientious as a counselor										
Takes constructive criticism well										
Is training an Intern										
Has trained the Intern to train										
Is supervising the new Intern										
The Intern's trainee can also train										
Has desire to become Zone Supervisor										
Recommended for Zone Supervisor										

INTERN EVALUATION FORM

TASK	LEVEL OF EXCELLENCE (10=HIGH; 1=LOW)									
	10	9	8	7	6	5	4	3	2	1
Has visited every Cell member at home										
Relates well to visitors										
Conscientiously "kins" new members										
Participates in discussions										
Brings unbelievers to Share Group										
Is taking, has taken, Shepherd training										
Coordinates visitation										
Personally makes visits										
Conducts Cell meetings effectively										
Well prepared to facilitate topics										
Effectively presents Share the Vision										
Sensitive to needs during discussions										
Lovingly cares for problemed people										
Leads Prayer Chain activity										
Prays consistently for members										
Keeps efficient records										
Conscientious as a counselor										
Takes constructive criticism well										
Is training an Intern										
Has trained the Intern to train										
Is supervising the new Intern										
The Intern's trainee can also train										
Has potential for Cell Leader										
Recommended for Cell Leader										

Prayer Chain

Name_____

Phones: (H)_____ (W)_____

Name_____

Phones: (H)_____ (W)_____

Name_____

Phones: (H)_____ (W)_____

Name_____

Phones: (H)_____ (W)_____

Name_____

Phones: (H)_____ (W)_____

Name_____

Phones: (H)_____ (W)_____

Name_____

Phones: (H)_____ (W)_____

Name_____

Phones: (H)_____ (W)_____

Name_____

Phones: (H)_____ (W)_____

CELL GROUP MEETING EVALUATION

Use this form with your Intern to evaluate the meeting.

SERVANT:

DATE: __/__/__   ATTENDANCE: _____

TOPIC:

What were the most significant events in the meeting?

What weaknesses or problems did you see in the meeting?

What did you learn that you did not know before?

What follow-up is needed?
(A visit, phone call, note of encouragement)

CELL GROUP PLANNING SHEET

SHEPHERD:

DATE OF MEETING: __/__/__

IN HOME OF:

ADDRESS:

DIRECTIONS:

PROJECT	ASSIGNED TO:	READY
FOOD		
INTRODUCE GUESTS		
ICE BREAKER		
PRAISE/WORSHIP		
DISCUSSION TOPIC		
SHARE THE VISION		
PRAYER TIME		

COMMENTS

Use this form for planning future Cell Group meetings with your Intern.

TOPIC PLANNING SHEET

Topic:_____ Date to be used: _/_/_

   Reason for using this topic at this time:

Ice Breaker: _____

Opening Question: _____

SCRIPTURES TO BE USED:

   1._____   2._____

After the group has focused on the topic, read scriptures, one at a time. After each one, ask: "How does this verse apply to our discussion?" If one verse does not bring forth a deep response from the group, move on to another one. When a scripture touches special needs within the group, let the discussion freely flow.

SHARE THE VISION TOPIC:

_____

If children are present in the families of the flock, how will you include them in the topic discussion, or what will you provide for them which will make the meeting profitable to them?

_____

_____

_____

Glossary of Terms

Affective Domain

The area of the human personality where our values are stored. There is no logic in this domain. It is impacted to some extent by cognitive information, but primarily by the experiences of life. In the Cell Group, the interaction between the members is a strong example of affective experiences. This domain requires a Facilitator, not a teacher.

Arrival Kit

The first module in "The Year of Equipping," dealing with the value system of the Kingdom of God and contrasting it with the values Christians typically use in day to day activity. Daily Growth Guides are provided for eleven weeks. Sponsor's Guide is in the back of the book.

Celebration

A gathering of all members of Cell groups within a region for an area wide time of worship, praise and Bible teaching; the largest assembly of a Cell Group Church.

Cell Group

A general term used to describe a Basic Christian Community which is under the guidance and authority of a larger church structure.

Cell Church

A nontraditional form of church life in which Cells of Christians meet in a special way in their homes for worship, edification, the evangelism of the unchurched, the bonding of believers, and their nurture and ministry to one another. It is a church which defines its Cells as "Basic Christian Communities," the building blocks of church life. Further gatherings of the Cells regionally are called "Congregations," and the full assembly of them is called a "Celebration."

Cognitive Domain

The domain of knowledge, requiring a teacher and students who desire to learn what the teacher transmits. In this area, logic exists. A person's value system is not found in the Cognitive Domain. (See also Affective and Psychomotor Domains.)

Congregation

A term used in the Cell Church movement to describe the clusters of Cells in a geographical area. Usually such a Congregation will gather from five to fifteen Cells, with each Cell averaging ten to twelve members. The Congregation may meet weekly or monthly. It gathers the Cells for Bible teaching, training, regional evangelism activities, or for an area ministry project. The Congregation is simply a collection of Cells and does not replace it as the basic building block of church life. In a large city, there may be many Congregations within a Cell Church.

Cover The Bible

A one year study course which reviews every chapter in the Bible, developed by TOUCH Outreach Ministries for use with unchurched persons. Five-minutes-a-day cassette recordings have been produced so the Cell member can go through the material in brief daily encounters. Equivalent to a Bible college survey of the Bible.

Enabler

See "Facilitator."

Equipper

Ephesians 4:11-16 teaches that all believers are ministers. As God gives spiritual gifts to all, He also provides gifted men to equip those with the gifts. Called "apostles, prophets, evangelists, pastors and teachers," the task of these men is to equip Christians for their ministries.

Facilitator

The work of the Cell Leader (also called Shepherd), who provides experiences for the group and passively guides the times of sharing in the gatherings. A Facilitator does not teach, does not control or dominate and does not respond to each comment made in a Cell Group.

Flock

A term used in *The Shepherd's Guidebook* to describe a Cell Group. (The Cell Leader is also called "Shepherd.")

House Church

In its pure definition, an indigenous group of Christians who meet in a home, or homes, for their activities and who have no affiliation with anyone else. The term is sometimes used to refer to a Cell Group, which is actually not a House Church. Rather, a Cell Group is a part of a larger context of Christians who meet in their homes but who are also banded together to create a movement within a city or region.

Ice Breakers

Describes the initial beginning activity in a small group, in which each person shares in turn. It "breaks the ice" in a gathering where some may feel insecure or ill at ease.

Intern

A trainee being prepared for ministry as a Cell Leader, also called a Shepherd. Every Cell Leader should have an Intern from the day a Cell Group is launched, because in approximately six months the group should be ready to multiply. At that point the

Intern will become a Cell Leader and work with one of the two new ones to be formed.

Interest Group

A segment of people reached by a Cell Group team specializing in a special problem or interest. Examples: single parents, joggers, alcoholics, parents of retarded children, LIFT Groups targeting unemployed persons.

Journey Guide

A booklet given to each person who enters a Cell Group. It helps the Shepherd create a guide to equip each Christian for ministry and growth. These equipping sessions are then provided in special modules to provide one year of basic training for ministry. A "Sponsor" is assigned to each incoming Cell member to assist them in their journey.

Kinning

The creation of family loyalty between members of a Cell Group.

Logo

A picture or drawing which has taken on a symbolical meaning, stirring both intellectual and emotional responses when viewed.

Ministry

A term used in the Cell Church to refer to the activity of every Christian and not just the ordained clergy, who are viewed as being the "equippers of the saints for the work of ministry."

Psychomotor Domain

The domain where motor skills are developed. An Instructor is necessary, usually a person who has already mastered the skills to be learned. Examples: learning to drive a car, guitar playing. It is possible to create Interest Groups in this domain.

Quaker Questions

An Ice Breaker often used in the first meeting of a small group. So named because it was used a century or more ago by Quakers in small villages to get acquainted with newcomers. They are fully described in *The Shepherd's Guidebook*.

Share Group

A small group for evangelism sponsored by a Cell Group. Three Cell members meet with persons who are not open to any religious activities. Training for Share Groups is provided by a trilogy of books: Building Bridges, Building Groups, and Building Awareness.

Shepherd

A term used to describe the ministry side of a Cell Leader's life.

Shepherd's Guidebook

A manual for equipping the Cell Group servant. Includes suggested formats for the meetings and forms useful in keeping records.

Small Group

A general term, usually referring to the activity of traditional churches where small groups are used for fellowship, discipleship, prayer, etc. Usually does not refer to a Cell Group, where the basic building block of church life is being created. Thus, the "Small Group" is only one of its many programs.

TOUCH

T.O.U.C.H. means 'TRANSFORMING OTHERS UNDER CHRIST'S HAND."

Touching Hearts Guidebook (THG)

An equipping module for those in a Cell Group who are learning how to share their faith using a special diagram based on John 3:16. (Replaces Knocking On Doors, Opening Hearts.)

TOUCH Outreach Ministries

Formed in the early 1970's in Houston, Texas, USA, this ministry is a consultant ministry focusing on Cell Churches within the United States. It is not a parachurch organization; instead, it is a ministry to serve Cell Churches.

"Type A" Unbelievers

Unbelievers who accept the Scriptures as valid, who have a Christian frame of reference and who are open to Bible study and the Christian message. They are reached through teams of Cell Group members.

"Type B" Unbelievers

Unbelievers who have no interest in the Scriptures, question their inspiration and have a limited frame of reference. They are not open to Bible Study, attending church services and may actually be hostile to the Christian message. They are cultivated through Share Groups and Interest Groups, evangelistic groups which build on topics of interest to unbelievers.